# THE
# Art of Being Agreeable.

BY

## MARGARET E. SANGSTER.

*" We pass this way but once."*

---

## Fredonia Books
## Amsterdam, The Netherlands

The Art of Being Agreeable

by
Margaret E. Sangster

ISBN: 1-58963-643-0

Reprinted from the 1897 edition,
Originally Published by the Christian Herald

Fredonia Books
Amsterdam, The Netherlands
http://www.fredoniabooks.com

In order to make original editions of historical works
available to scholars at an economical price, this
facsimile of the original edition of 1897 is
reproduced from the best available copy and has
been digitally enhanced to improve legibility, but the
text remains unaltered to retain historical
authenticity.

THIS BOOK IS DEDICATED,

WITH THE LOVE OF MANY SWEET YEARS

TO

SUSAN PORTER DU BOIS.

# CONTENTS.

|  | PAGE |
|---|---|
| The Art of Being Agreeable | 7 |
| Manners on Life's Journey | 13 |
| Regard for the Rights of Others | 22 |
| Even-Tempered Wives | 37 |
| Sunshiny Husbands | 49 |
| Parents and Children | 58 |
| Over-Sensitive People | 71 |
| The Child's Point of View | 82 |
| The Social Relations of Boys and Girls | 93 |
| The Daughter at Home. | 97 |
| When we go Visiting | 108 |
| In Co-Operative Housekeeping | 118 |
| When Fortune Favors | 127 |
| When Times are Hard | 136 |
| Hopefulness | 145 |
| Interesting People | 152 |
| Agreeable in Illness | 160 |
| Agreeable in Old Age | 170 |
| The Givers of Advice | 181 |
| Men, Women and Society | 186 |
| Grown-Up Sons and Daughters | 195 |
| Tact | 204 |
| Purity of Speech | 211 |
| Deference to the Old | 218 |

# 6 *Contents.*

|                              | PAGE |
|------------------------------|------|
| A Talk about Clothes         | 227  |
| Out of the Procession        | 236  |
| The Good Listener            | 239  |
| Teachers and Scholars        | 245  |
| Rest when You are Tired      | 254  |
| The Money Bag                | 271  |
| Correspondence               | 277  |
| Some Charming Examples       | 287  |
| The Very Best                | 301  |
| Fine Manners                 | 306  |

# THE

# ART OF BEING AGREEABLE.

---

## THE ART OF BEING AGREEABLE.

Into the minutest details of our daily life,
into our hours of prosperity and adversity
alike, in seasons of calm weather, and in
hours of storm and stress, enters the need of
holding one's self well in hand, of control-
ling circumstances, in short, of being agreeable. Just as the price of excellence in
ther departments is vigilance, study, and
incessant endeavor, so in this finest of arts
he or she who would be eminent, must make
the matter a subject of conscientious effort.
As at West Point or Annapolis, the cadet is
drilled and drilled and drilled, till he emerges,
after the specified period of laborious training, a model of deportment, and a man of
various resources; so in our homes, our
offices, our shops, and our farms and facto-
ries and streets, we must day by day submit
to repression here, and practice expression
there, if we would fully master the art of
being agreeable. To be this signifies to be

(7)

pleasing, to be polite, to accept another's
point of view, to regard another's limitations, to live on the whole, according to
the Sermon on the Mount.

Wherever people are gathered in large
numbers, as at a college, for instruction ; in a
great house of business, where many are
employed, and the fidelity of each accrues
to the advantage of all ; in a church, where
the members have a common interest ; in
any organization in which the individual
must subordinate himself for the benefit of the
entire body,—there it is necessary that the art
of being agreeable should flourish. For, as
one screw loose may serve to sink a ship, and
one loose plank in the foundation may cause
the mill to totter and fall, so one cantanker-
ous, unreasonable, ill-conditioned and disagreeable person may effectually demoralize
the entire band. Nothing works more un-
failingly than the leaven of evil, and a little
leaven leaveneth the whole lump.

In the closer quarters of the family, where
we are interdependent and the temper of
one may make the prevailing atmosphere of
the household joyous or sad for days together, it is still more incumbent on us to
cultivate amiable dispositions and habit-
ual unselfishness. The essence of being
agreeable is being like our Master, of whom it
is written that, " He pleased not Himself."

Ian Maclaren tells us, in the " Mind of the
Master." that "Love is the destruction of

sin," because love connects instead of isolat-
ing. No one can be envious, avaricious,
hard-hearted, no one can be gross, sensual,
unclean, if he loves. Love is the death of
all bitter and unholy moods of the soul, because love lifts the man out of himself and
teaches him to live in another. Jesus did
not think it needful to eulogize the virtues ;
it would have been a work of supereroga-
tion when he had insisted upon love. Jesus
has changed ethics from a crystal that can
only grow by accretion into a living plant
that flowers in its season. He exposed the
negative principle of morals in His empty
house, swept and garnished ; He vindicated
the positive principle in His house held by
a strong man armed.

The individualism of selfishness is the
disintegrating force which has cursed this
world, segregating the individual, and rend-
ing society to pieces. The altruism of love
is the consolidating force which will save
the world, reconciling man to his fellows,
and recreating society.

We are constantly impressed in our study
of the life of Christ when He wore our flesh
and dwelt among us, with the importance
He attached to love. Over and over again
we are told to love one another. The New
Testament is fragrant with the perfume of
this broken alabaster box ; we are com-
manded to a blessed altruism which prefers
the neighbor to one's self. St. Paul says,

"Love suffereth long and is kind, love vaunteth not itself, love thinketh no evil." "Love is the fulfilling of the law." St. John. pleads with us tenderly, "Little children, love one another, for love is of God." Away back, centuries before Christ came to the earth, we find Isaiah writing sentences steeped with tenderest love, language laboring to show how the Father looks upon us in infinite fondness and with continual complacency, pitying and forgiving our sins, blotting them out, making us, though red like crimson, whiter than snow, and crowning everything by those immortal words, "I have called thee by thy name; thou art mine."

Does it seem like a descent from that which is holy to that which is common, when, in the same breath, with the love of God, we speak of being agreeable? Not so; for to be agreeable is to sacrifice selfish inclination, to crucify exclusiveness, to be neither brutal nor brusque, but to make this one little life which is given us to live in, this sphere of service, as perfect and as beautiful as we can.

> " We may not climb the Heavenly steeps
>     To bring the Lord Christ down ;
>  In vain we scarch the lowest deeps,
>     For Him no depths can drown.
>
> " But warm, sweet, tender, even yet
>     A present help is He ;
>  And faith has still its Olivet,
>     And love its Galilee.

> "The healing of His seamless dress
>    Is by our beds of pain;
> We touch Him in life's storm and stress,
>    And we are whole again.
>
> "O Lord and Master of us all!
>    Whate'er Thy name or sign,
> We own Thy sway, we hear Thy call,
>    We test our lives by Thine."

All this of necessity puts the art of being agreeable on a lofty plane. When we shall have reached this, the world will be a very different place.

To a fair woman, who had gone to live in one of the crowded and gloomy tenement-house districts of the East Side in New York city, a girl, accustomed her life long to hard knocks and much unkindness, said, "Do you mean to tell me that you won't gain anything by coming down here? Isn't there any money in it for you and your friends?"

Assured that money was the last thing thought of, she said musingly, "It's the first time I ever found folks just kind and nice with nothing back of it, and I believe in them, they are so good." When we can put the art of being agreeable to such uses as this, we are indeed taking into the temples our vessels of silver and vessels of gold, and burning before God our sweet-smelling incense.

You know how an unused house wears out and falls to decay,—roof and walls and weatherboards and shingles growing rotten in the damp, and falling to pieces; nails loosening, rain and snow driving in before long.    A lived-in house, with a large family treading its stairs and passages, is not so soon a prey to the ravages of time.

So, too, the rich garment of silk or wool or fur, left unworn in the closet or wardrobe wears out ; the moths eat it, the rich surface is fretted by time.

In like manner, we must use our good-breeding and keep our politeness in repair. As we live among our friends and kindred, as we have commerce with all sorts and conditions of men, we shall cultivate the art of being agreeable, always bearing in mind that "Love is the fulfilling of the law," and that "we pass this way but once."

"Abou Ben Adhem, may his tribe increase,
  Awoke one night from a deep dream of peace,"

and saw, you recollect, an angel writing with a golden pen, the names of those who loved the Lord.

"And is mine one?" he asked.   "Nay," said the angel.   "I pray thee then," said Adhem, "write me as one who loves his fellow-men."

When next the angel came, we know the sequel, for

"Lo! Ben Adhem's name led all the rest."

## MANNERS ON LIFE'S JOURNEY.

Perhaps people reveal their dispositions and characters more unconsciously when they are travelling than at any other time. When we are among our own people, and where everybody knows us, we are more or less under a certain restraint ; but away from home and in a crowd of strangers with unfamiliar faces on every hand, the temptation to be less courteous than ordinarily sometimes assails the most amiable.

When we see people pushing roughly in a crowd to get the foremost place, or insisting in a railway train on opening a window or closing it, oblivious to the comfort of those around, then we do not need to go far to label these characters as at least very selfish.

Not long ago I saw an elderly woman obstruct a throng of people anxious to get home after a busy day, by handing the man at a ticket-desk a five-dollar bill.   Out of this five-dollar bill were to be taken two little tickets worth five cents.  She counted her change deliberately twice, while a long string of men and women eagerly waited their turn, and could not get it because she maintained her ground with perfect com-

posure. This was on her part a great
breach of good manners on the road.

In the very small matter of always providing one's self with small change, so that
on ferries and cars and elsewhere one shall
occasion no delay, there is room for improvement in many. A sweet girl said the
other day, "I always take pains to have
nickels and dimes with me, because I fancy
that conductors have a great deal to worry
them, and I do not like to add to the incon-
veniences of their lot." This young woman
obliged not only the conductors, but her
fellow-passengers and all with whom she
came in contact by this instinct of thoughtfulness upen the road.

A mother travelling with small children
and having perhaps a journey of many hours
before her, is greatly aided by the thoughtfulness of other passengers who do not look
angry or disturbed if a baby happens to
cry, who perhaps produce, as I saw a kind
man do not long ago, a picture-book for the
amusement of restless little boys, and who
in many ways show that they have consideration and regard for one who has her
hands full.

One day this summer, while sitting in
church at Northfield, where Mr. Moody was
preaching, I heard him say to a young
mother about to take her infant out of the
building, "Madam, do not disturb yourself
on my account. I can preach louder than a

baby can cry, and nobody is troubled by the
restlessness of that little child. If any lady
or gentleman wishes to go, I am quite willing to give my permission, but I like to see
little children with their mothers in the house
of God."

Perhaps one reason why mothers keep
little children away from church so much as
they do, is that they fear the little ones will
disturb those around them. A good rule for
us all would be never to allow ourselves to
show any lack of tranquillity on account of
the presence of children. What would the
world be with no little children in it? It
would seem as if suddenly clouds had come
over the sunshine, and the birds and the
flowers had flown and vanished away. We
owe a good deal of our joy and gladness in
this world to the dear little people who keep
us in remembrance of our own childhood,
and we never, on a journey or elsewhere,
should manifest any dislike to their presence.

But our manners upon the road are concerned with something more than the mere
travelling about. How many of us take
time to give a clear and explicit direction to
the person who stops us to ask the way to
an unfamiliar point? How often do we take
pains to show courtesy and attention to an
entire stranger? A friend travelling recently
in the South told me of his surprise and delight at having a man absolutely go a whole
hour's journey out of his way, in order to

show him a point of interest and a beautiful
view. Few of us take the time to be thus
kind and neighborly in a world where, after
all, there is nothing lovelier than the spirit
of good neighborhood and kindness.

It used to be the boast of all Americans
that no woman ever had to stand in a public
conveyance ; the moment a lady appeared
somebody would rise and courteously press
on her his seat. I did once hear a funny
story of an immensely stout lady who appeared in the door of a car, and as the sight
of her three hundred pounds blocked the
way, one gentleman rose and said impres-
sively, "I will be one of three to give that
lady a seat." This story is probably fiction.
But I have seen three rise at once to offer a
seat to a woman whose avoirdupois gave
her no claim on their attention.

We all know that a change has come over
the manners of our countrymen in this particular, and it is no longer true that mere
womanhood gives a claim upon the stronger
sex for attention in this way. Let us not
find fault. Very often the man is as tired
and as much in need of the seat as is the
woman ; and if the respect is still shown to
silver hairs, and, as almost universally, to
the woman who carries in her arms a child,
we must not complain.

Also a very strong point in good manners
is that no service shall be accepted from
anybody without a prompt expression of

thanks. To see a women sink into a seat a man has resigned for her without so much as a look of gratitude, is to feel that he is justified in never again denying himself for the sake of such ingrates as women sometimes prove themselves to be.

Our manners upon the road include, let me say here, the prompt acknowledgment of all the courtesies. If we receive a present, however trifling it may be, it is a token of goodwill and a proof that we have been remembered, and it should be at once or with as little delay as possible, acknowledged by a note of thanks or else by a very full verbal expression of our pleasure. We should never economize in thanks; they may be as profuse as possible—the more so the better.

It is a beautiful trait of some people to keep in mind the birthdays of their friends. They do this perhaps by a little note in a birthday book, or in some way their memories are jogged at the right moment, and when an anniversary comes around it is met by a lovely souvenir from the hand of affection. So, too, Easter and Christmas come, with their pleasant opportunities of showing our friends how much we love them.

There is nothing more delightful than to receive an unexpected present. A wife is always made very happy by a gift from her husband, the more so if it comes at a

2

time when there is no particular occasion
for it except in his love; and between
brothers and sisters, children and their parents, no sweeter thing in life can be found
than the interchange of loving gifts at holiday and other times.

Flowers play an important part in the
courtesies of life. It is always appropriate
to give a friend a flower. They go to the
sick room with their messages of cheer.
You may send them to your friend who
is in sorrow; when no word can be said
to comfort her, the rose or the lily comes
into her room and lays a soft caressing
hand upon her aching heart.

So it is quite worth while to let the children early begin the cultivation of flowers.
How dearly we remember the days when
we ourselves had little garden-beds which
were our own and where we were allowed,
when we pleased, to sow the seeds, pull up
the weeds, and gather flowers for the
father's buttonhole or the mother's plate in
the morning. Every little child should have
a garden of its very own, where there will
be the utmost liberty to do precisely what it
pleases.

In the country the child may romp at
will among the daisies and clover, and come
home from rambles with hands overflowing
with bloom; but in the city the children
are limited to back-yards with narrow
flower borders around a plot of green grass.

Even here some mothers manage to have little gardens for the children, where they may cultivate pinks, verbenas, sweet peas, petunias, four o'clock, and those darlings of all children, the little pansies with their sweet faces. With great pride the children present the father with a flower for his buttonhole, or bring a blossom to adorn the breakfast-table or lay beside the mother's plate. Part of all the childish training should be to give pleasure to others, and perhaps there is no way in which pleasure is more easily given than by the bestowment of flowers.

Some young ladies who started a gospel mission in New York last summer had their rooms profusely decorated on their opening night with peonies and wonderful roses— great masses of bloom from an old-fashioned country garden. What was their amazement to find that the children who poured in to hear their songs and share the enjoyment of the first evening rushed upon the flowers like an invading army, and in a few moments stripped the rooms of every single blossom that was there. They went out into the street with their arms full, and although a little later they learned to respect the property which was not theirs, their first almost savage onset showed how starved their lives had been for beauty.

One can never go through the crowded streets down-town in New York carrying

flowers without a petition on every hand
from the children, ragged, thin and sorrow-
ful-looking, who throng upon one's steps
asking to please give them the flowers. So
that as we go through life we may both
theoretically and practically add to its
pleasure by considering flowers not so
much a superfluity as a necessity. Perhaps we can start flower missions of our
own.

A friend attempted once to do good to
some poor people who had been the despair
of every one who had tried to help them.
The first time she went to their door it was
slammed in her face. The second time she
went carrying with her a beautiful rose,
and as the door was opened and the mother
put out her hard and sullen face it softened
at the sight of the flower, the door was
opened, the lady entered, and with her
came a new era of peace and prosperity to
that home, because she came to it as one of
God's angels ; and from the day that she
gained admission she was the helper and
friend of all beneath the roof.

In a recently published article by Professor
Wyckoff, in one of the numbers of *Scribner's
Magazine*, there was an interesting account
of how this gentleman disguised himself as
a tramp and set out to look for work. He
asked only work ; he refused to accept
alms ; not even a morsel of food would he
take unless he worked for it. He had

burned his ships behind him, and carried
with him not even a cent of money.

It is interesting and also painful to learn
that the majority of the people to whom
Professor Wyckoff applied treated him with
scorn and contumely ; that suspicion and
indifference, if not contempt, met him at
every step ; that he had to conciliate the
farmer's wives as well as the dogs, and that
he found the way of an unskilled laborer
beset with a thousand needless hardships.

Surely upon the road of life we need not
make things harder for those whose lot is
already a sufficiently difficult one to bear.
Even to tramps and beggars, who are out-
casts from home and have no roof above
their heads, we may show Christian kindness. When the day comes that no one
looks down upon another, and all are
anxious for Christ's sake to help those who
are sad, way-worn and distressed, we shall
see a different state of things in this world
of God's.

## REGARD FOR THE RIGHTS OF OTHERS.

Perhaps among the minor trials of life none more persistently forces itself upon our notice than the disregard of many good people for the rights of others. They give trouble when to do so is needless. For instance, a busy friend of mine said to me one day : "A great deal of my precious time is taken up in going after my husband and setting the house in order after he leaves it in the morning. No matter how tidy it may be at his return in the evening, he again manages to give my drawing-room, sitting-room and library an appearance of having been swept by a cyclone. One traces him all over the house by the things he has heedlessly dropped ; and the worst of it is that the children imitate him and expect from me the same sort of attention in putting aside their clothing, books and papers which I willingly give to their father, but which I rebel against in their case."

In this instance, the wife should have early made a stand for herself and insisted that her good man should, to some extent, respect the rules of good order and put away things where they belonged without waiting for her willing hands to serve him. A very sensible mother of my acquaintance always begins with her little people when they are very small and has a set of graduated hooks suited to their sizes so that each one, as he or she comes from play, may hang up coat and hat, while in a closet conveniently placed, there are special compartments for every child. The little ones are allowed great freedom in the use of their things, but each child must individualize its own property, and they are not allowed indiscriminate use of what belongs to one another. Under certain restrictions they may lend their possessions, though lending is not encouraged, and they are being brought up with a strict feeling in regard to property rights, and a sort of responsibility is inculcated by the very care which they are obliged to take of their garments and playthings. This care is especially insisted upon with reference to books, and each child is taught what it would be well for all to learn early in life,— real reverence for the printed page. Books in that home are not allowed to lie open when their owners leave them, nor are leaves recklessly turned down, nor precious volumes suffered to lie out of doors and become rain-soaked. When these children grew up they will be decidedly agreeable people to live with, because they will have learned to care for their own rights and to respect the rights of others. In some families nobody seems to possess anything. Daughters rush to their mother's bureau drawers and seize upon her gloves, handkerchiefs, and neckwear as it suits their convenience. Mother appears to be a sort of person on whom the children may make predatory excursions as often as they like. In consequence, she never knows upon what she may count if, poor lady, she is asked for a visit or sets out upon a round of calls herself. A girl whom I knew, a dear lovely creature to whom her friends were all devoted, had the one unfortunate habit of helping herself at will to her sister's things whenever she happened to fancy something of hers as nicer than her own. One day, she was taken very ill quite suddenly, and was for some hours in very great danger. As a matter of course the family anxiety was great, and just when every one was wrought up to concert-pitch, the sufferer created a diversion and assured them that she was getting better by exclaiming : "Oh, Mary, if I only live, I solemnly promise that I will never take your collars and cuffs again !" At that moment, the promise was not desired, but later, Mary did not fail to remind the delinquent that it had been made. In the interesting "True Life of George Washington," by Paul Leicester Ford, we chance upon a little incident which shows how a hundred years ago our great general was annoyed by the heedlessness of a young relative who was for a time a member of his household. Of this niece, Harriot, he tells that her "chief falling was no disposition . . . to be careful of her cloathes," which were "dabbed about in every hole and corner and her best things always in use," so that Washington said, "She costs me enough!" To her uncle she wrote on one occasion : "How shall I apologize to my dear and Honor'd for intruding on his goodness so soon again, but being sensible for your kindness to me, which I shall ever remember with the most heartfelt gratitude, induces me to make known my wants. I have not had a pair of stays since I first came here: if you could let me have a pair I should be very much obliged to you, and also a hat and a few other articles. I hope my dear Uncle will not think me extravagant for really I take as much care of my cloathes as I possibly can." A writer in the *Evening Post* recently advises parents to be more careful than they usually are in the early instructions to little children with regard to the care of property, particularly that which does not belong to them. The article is so admirable a lesson that I quote it :

"To enforce upon children regard for other people and their property, to punish, by restraint or deprivation of certain pleasures, injuries to furniture, flowers, books, walls, anything which they ought not to handle— is merely to make a groundwork of decent

regard for other people's rights.   I saw two
children, eight or ten years old, tear up the
larger part of a bit of shrubbery just coming
into bloom, and throw the blossoms on the
ground, while their mothers watched them
from the veranda in complacent quiet.
'They were having such a good time with
those wild flowers.' The mistress of the
house absolutely turned pale when she saw
the destruction ; the shrubs were coming
into bloom for the first time.   The little girls
were not even told to gather up the litter
they had made, but left walks and lawn un-
tidy, and rushed off to find something else
to tear up and destroy.

"To learn to respect the perfection of
things is of infinite value to a child.   If it is
a flower, to shelter and try to keep it alive.
never wantonly to pluck and fling away a
blossom ; if it is a book, not to deface or
mar it ; if it is a wall, not to mark or deface
it ; if it is a smooth-rolled lawn, not to litter it with rubbish or deface it with wheel-
marks.   To learn to wait patiently ; all their
lives long they will give thanks for having
been taught how to do this.   How many a
pleasant talk has been interrupted, how
many an otherwise helpful visit has been
lost by a teasing, pulling child, tormenting
its mother either to listen to its demands or
to go somewhere.

"The whole of its life lies in what the
child learns of these things, and it must

either grow into selfish manhood, or womanhood, or have the evil beaten out by the hard and bitter teachings of the world in which it was meant to be happy and useful, rather than to begin thus late to learn that we cannot live unto ourselves.

"Better that the children never knew a word of any language but their own, that they were devoid of many society accomplishments, than that they should fail to learn faithful obedience, respect for the rights of others, and primary self-restraint, which is the foundation of all pleasant intercourse between human beings of every age.

"There is no reason why children should not be a joy wherever they go; a refreshment, even an amusement to their world-tired elders, to whom their innocent pleasures, their spontaneous, unaffected merriment, their original and ingenious thoughts are like a new and diverting book; and surely to many forms of grief no tenderness is as soothing as the love and caress of a dear child.

"If they are looked upon as pests and nuisances, if the nervous shrink from their shrill screams and continued fretfulness, the delicate from their rude ways, and the refined from their destructiveness, it is the fault of their mothers, not the children.

"Put the culture of the heart and character of your children far above the improvement of their minds.

"It is easier to yield than to show a child that he cannot be indulged ; it is far easier to quiet a restless little spirit with a forbidden plaything than to insist on his amusing himself legitimately ; but every day the mother or nurse who would grieve sincerely that any lack of care or forethought had entailed a bump or bruise, will permit him without regret to acquire habits which make him a trial wherever he goes, and which only the rod of life's hard discipline can remove.

"The subtle form of selfishness which causes this lamentable result hides itself away under many coverings, but in the end the finished work is the same ; the distasteful, annoying, obnoxious child owes his condition to his mother, and she has been cruel to him."

Primarily, the blame for a careless trampling upon the rights of others lies at the door of parents. If they begin with children in their early years they can easily train them into whatever habits they please. Even heredity, strong as it is, yields to constant, gentle and relentless training. None of us would quite approve of the method of Madame Beck, whose continual *surveillance* of her scholars and family so horrified her English governess in Charlotte Bronte's wonderful story *Villette.* But there is a quality of genuine common sense in her observation about one little daughter, that "This child needs to be very constantly watched." We should

not watch our children in the indirect and
stealthy way adopted by this mother, whose
Jesuitical training made her see no harm in
playing the part of a spy, but mothers cannot be too constantly vigilant, for it is
true that time is constantly going on, that
the child is growing out of our hands, and
that by and by we may ruefully say as did
one of old : "While Thy servant was busy
here and there, he was gone." People who
are agreeable members of a family do not
call attention to every little defect in the
fit of a gown ; they do not tell you that your
bonnet is unbecoming, that you are looking
ill to-day or that the frock or gown which
has just come home to you from the dressmaker would better suit your grandmother
than yourself. I have sometimes found that
the people who say such things are quite
willing to borrow the very finery which they
discover is not appropriate to its original
owner. The whole matter of borrowing,
of family criticism and of family jars, is very
closely related.

We cannot expect people to live in a
home in the severe isolation of ivory balls
laid side by side, but there is much friction
which could be avoided, and a great deal of
it comes from failure to exercise the same
care in regard to relatives which we always
show in our intercourse with strangers.

From a very early period in life young
people should practice perfect honesty, so

far as financial transactions in the household are concerned. If Jennie asks Arthur
to lend her five or ten cents, or Arthur seeks
a small accommodation of that sort from
Kate, there should be the utmost precision
in returning the amount as promptly as
possible. In fact, the ease and charm of
life everywhere are dependent upon foundation stones of integrity and honor. This
naturally leads to a reminder that people
should be prompt in settling small obliga-
tions. A poor laundress said to me, not long
ago : "I have the greatest respect for Dr.
——,"—mentioning a well-known clergyman. "I used to work frequently in his
family and I have often heard him say
at the end of the day: 'Mamma, do not
let Sophy go home without her money, even
if she is coming again to-morrow. You
know she has a house full of children to care
for !'" Entire exactness in small things leads
to good management in larger ones. Never
should one take liberties in any instance
with funds intrusted to his or her care. A
young lady said to me one day : "I am
in the greatest perplexity and trouble. I
am Treasurer of the Benevolent Society of
our church, and I had last week in my care
about $70.00. A friend came in and begged
me to lend him the money, saying he would
give it back to me the next day and that it
would be just as safe in his hands as it was
in mine. I foolishly and weakly yielded to

his importunities and lent him the money,
and now there comes a request from him to
allow him to keep it still longer, and altogether I am very much worried." The
young lady made the mistake which we all
make when we treat as our own that which
really is given to us in trust. We have no
right to lend that which does not belong to
us. In her case, she was compelled to ask
her father to make good the amount she
had allowed to pass from her hands to
those of an irresponsible person. People
frequently forget that funds with which they
are intrusted are in no sense their own,
that they are simply stewards, and that as
stewards they must render an account of
their stewardship. In a lesser way, some
of us need to remind ourselves that it is
possible to be too obliging when we are
asked to lend, just for a few days, to an insistent friend the volume which another
friend has lent to us—a very indefensible
piece of business on all sides. The party
of the first part in this transaction is in the
hands of the party of the second part, and
she of the third part has no right nor privilege in the matter whatever. The whole
question of borrowing books is fraught with
interrogation points which bristle on every
side. I do not think a really agreeable person ever voluntarily borrows a friend's book,
unless where there is great intimacy. The
very doing so proves the person disagreeable;

for, as a rule, people are not more willing, underneath the surface, to lend their books than they are to lend their shoes, or gloves or petticoats or mantillas or their best bonnets. Few people have the courage of their convictions in this matter.

Not one person in a thousand will adopt the course of a gentleman who, having a large library, told me that he had long ago made it a point never to lend a book from a set. "I do not object," said he courteously, to a neighbor who desired the loan of one volume from a set of sixty, "to your taking the entire series of works if you will kindly send a wheelbarrow for them, but I never allow a set of books to be broken." Those of us who have yawning gaps in our libraries, made by the absence of certain numbers in beloved editions, or whose favorite authors have come home stained and worn and in evil case from the treatment they have received at the hands of our acquaintances, can but admire the strength of mind which forms and adheres to such a resolution.

In most towns there are public libraries from which one may freely draw books, and in many small places there are profitable book clubs which allow volumes to go for a stated time from hand to hand and house to house. Thoroughly well-bred persons hesitate to ask the loan of a book even from an intimate friend or a kinsman : and if one ac-

cepts such a favor, it behooves one to take
the very greatest care of this property while
it is with her, and to return it uninjured at
the earliest practicable opportunity, not
even permitting it to pass in her family from
hand to hand, since the loan of a book is an
individual transaction not intended to be
shared by a half dozen people.

And now, having said all this, let me add
that, notwithstanding it, a very lovely way
of doing good is to keep a certain number
of books by one for the special purpose of
lending. One may have books which she
knows will give great pleasure, and which
she deliberately sesolves to send about
among her friends or among young people
whom she knows. If she determines to do
this and puts her inclination into practice,
she may be a true benefactor, and there may
be among those to whom she shows this
kindness, some who may rise up and call
her blessed. In a country house up the
Hudson, there dwell two dear and honored
old people whose children and grandchildren have gone forth from them into the
world, and who, in a long life, have found
much pleasure in their large library of choice
books. One section of this library they
have set apart for the pleasure of their
neighbors, and any one who wishes may
freely come at any time and procure a book,
the only stipulation in the case being that the
name of the volume, the date of its with-

3

drawal from the shelf and the name of the borrower shall be entered by him or her in a little book which, with a pencil beside it, hangs conspicuously beside one of the shelves. The books are not enclosed by glass or locked up like prisoners ; the door of the library is always open, and no formula of asking or of thankfulness in return is expected, but it is taken for granted that whoever shares the kindness and courtesy of these always considerate people, shall enter the names and dates punctiliously in the book. They are also asked on returning the volume to set down in the book the fact that they have done so, and to add the date of the return.

Umbrellas, for some occult reason, curiously subtle, have from time immemorial seemed to be common property, and many persons, otherwise exceedingly thoughtful, forget when the sun shines to return the umbrella which was so welcome a boon in the rain.    Let us make a little mental note of this, and if we are wise we shall not behave as did two young women who were temporary guests of a courteous matron in whose house they were overtaken by a sudden summer tempest.    In order to save their delicate gowns from injury, she pressed upon them rain cloaks and overshoes and fitted them up with umbrellas, and sent them forth to their homes thoroughly fortified against the tempest.    The next day, with-

out a note or a word of thanks, her property
came back to her. The cloaks were encrust-
ed with mud, spattered and stained up to
the knees ; the overshoes were a sight to behold and one of the umbrellas had a broken
rib. My friend said to me quite calmly,
after she had spent a morning in restoring
her property to its pristine freshness and had
sent the umbrella away for repair : "I have
always heard that people show their breeding
in such little matters as this. You know as
well as I that although these girls have had
every advantage, their parents came from a
very ordinary class of people in the first
place and they have never had the fine feeling which the gentleman or the lady to the
manor born cannot help having." The re-
flection upon the parents may have been
unjust. I was inclined to think that only
girlish thoughtlessness was in the case, but
my friend, an aristocrat to her finger tips,
has never changed her view of the matter.

If one is a guest in a strange house, the
obligation to keep one's own room in order
and not to leave one's personal belongings
lying about loosely everywhere is much
greater than if one be in one's own home.
It happened to a lady, who is a fastidious
housekeeper, to entertain some time ago, a
number of young people who had come to
her town as delegates to a Christian Endeavor Convention. It was understood that
they were going to meetings from morning

to night, and that they were in a strange place where many novelties attracted their attention, but that was no excuse for their leaving their rooms in a state of untidiness which was simply frightful to behold. In one case, a youth who had the tongue of an Apollos, and whose eloquent speech and practical administration of affairs in convention did him great honor, managed to break a costly ewer, and said nothing about the fact that he had done so. He left towels and soiled and clean clothing strewn about his room in wild confusion ; and a cake of toilet soap was found lying under the bed after he had gone home. "Deliver me," said the lady, "from ever entertaining such guests again." "Let not your good be evil spoken of," is a motto it would be well for us all to adopt, and particularly when we are representing bodies of Christian people and are away from home. Let us be more than fastidious in the way in which we treat the effects and the homes to which we have access.

## EVEN-TEMPERED WIVES.

From a very early period we begin to
make the kind of people we are going to be.
When the little girl stamps her foot and flies
into a fury because she cannot have just
what she wants, she is laying the foundation for much unhappiness in future life.
Evenness of temper is a different thing from
evenness of manner, but the habit of repress-
ing the hasty speech, of being careful of
how we look and of what we say, contributes
really to the gentle temper which makes the
charm of life.

I have lately been staying under the roof
of a fair woman, around whom rises a large
family of grown-up sons and daughters, all
of whom adore her. In the days when her
ten children were coming and the nest was
always crowded, this mother was sometimes
tired, and sometimes her courage failed. She
had many days when she did not feel quite
up to the mark, and sometimes it seemed as
if she would not have strength for all that
God meant her to do and to be.

But to-day, as her stalwart sons and beautiful daughters crowd around the little

mother, she is marvellously young and fair
and sweet, and one of her children said to
me, "I have always taken my mother as an
example because her temper has been under
such control and always so even ; we have
always known where to find her and what
to depend upon."

Women are subject to many little flurries
and gusts, owing to their peculiarly sensitive
organization and to the fact that they are
less able to escape from small interruptions
than men are ; but still the control of one's
temper is largely a matter of will, and somehow the mother sets the pace and makes the
music of the home.   Baby's skies are mother's eyes, and when the mother is cheerful,
happy and considerate, the household ba-
rometer stands at fair weather and there is
little danger of storm or tempest under that
roof.

Then, too, the habit of being even-tempered and gentle under the multitudinous
cares and thick-crowding interruptions of
the day tend to give a woman a certain
strength which enables her to stand up under
the larger burdens when they come.   Mr.
Moody said to me one day last summer,
"Worry is the woman's sin," and I thought
he was right.   It is much harder for women
to keep from forecasting to-morrow than it
would be if they were not so incessantly
occupied with the round of petty cares, and
with drudgery which seemingly has no end.

For this reason, whenever it is possible, the mother should take a little vacation and escape, so far as she can, if only for a day or two, from the state of circumstances which usually are about her, into another state which will give her a different outlook. This is precisely the thing which mothers find it hardest to do. They say "I cannot be spared; everything would go to pieces if I should leave my post." Sometimes they boast that for years they have not had a holiday. Sometimes they refuse to take such little outings as might be managed, from a mistaken sense of duty and of responsibility.

But we have all seen how wonderfully a mother picks up health and strength and gets back her lost youth when she is persuaded in some happy day to leave her cares in the hands of a sister or an older daughter, to put on a pretty new gown and go away with her husband for a visit extending over some days or weeks. From the moment the mother leaves the house and the cars whirl her away she begins growing younger and a certain spring comes back to her life which she thought had left it forever.

Children could sometimes manage better than they do in their mothers' interests if they only realized how much the mothers stand in need of petting, and how much easier it would be for a mother if she could drop her responsibilities for a little while. It would be well for all of us if there were more demonstration in our love. Very many of us are like the good deacon in "Old-town Folks," who having once upon a time explained to his wife that he loved her, from that time on he never thought it necessary to allude to the fact again.

Some of our dear deceased friends would be very much astonished should they come back and discover how deeply they are mourned, because certainly it never was made apparent to them while they were here that they were of very much account to anybody ; and yet it is more from want of thought that evil is wrought than from intention, and the mother should take to herself the thought that she owes something to her own nature and to her own possibilities of development, as well as to her children and her friends.

The fault against which wives need to guard is an excessive candor. They are apt to speak a little too plainly, and it would be quite as well in the interest of happiness if they would retain something of the deference in their behavior which it was their joy to show the man of their choice during the courting days. Men respond very quickly to caresses and sentiment, and even a gray-haired father, or a strong man whom no one suspects of yearning for expressed fondness, is the better for having his wife put her arms around him and tell him how much she loves and admires him.

A little formality in our household intercourse is not a bad thing. The great danger of intimacy — and no relation is so intimate as that of the wedded life — is that we cease to be sufficiently on guard. People are under no restraint; they say the thing that comes first. Sometimes a woman, yielding to a little mood of depression or unhappiness or to a disappointment, utters words which rankle in a man's memory like poisonous stings. Words may wound, may be keen-edged as a sword or blunt as a club, and so may leave a stab or a bruise.

Really, when we come to think of it, most of our friction in this life is quite unnecessary, and nearly all domestic jars resolve themselves into much ado about nothing. Looking back over the quarrel which was so petty, yet which hurt at the time, we say how wise it would have been to have kept silent; how much unhappiness would have been saved had the matter simply been allowed to drift by without notice.

Solomon, who had great experience with women, seems to have had an especial terror of one with a sharp tongue, for he says, "It is better to live in a corner of the housetop than with a brawling woman in a wide house."

I once heard a very sweet bit of counsel given to one who was apt to let herself be

easily perturbed. The person to whom she
spoke said, "My dear, whenever you feel
agitated and out of sorts and ready to give
way to ill-temper, say to yourself, very
quietly and tranquilly 'The Lord is in His
holy temple ; let all the earth keep silence before Him.'" A little thought will show the
meaning of this, which is simply that we
all, if we are believers in the love of the
Heavenly Father and in the indwelling of
the Redeemer, are temples in which the
Lord may make his abode. If we have
asked him to dwell in us and to shine out of
us, it is certainly very unfit and unbecoming that we should be at the mercy of every
little mood. Those who walk with Christ
consciously always walk serenely.

In order to be entirely agreeable and even-
tempered, we women must not attempt to
do too much in one day. There are little
frocks to be made for the sweet little daughter of the house, and the temptation is to
add frill to frill and puff to puff and flounce
to flounce until the modest little slip which
would have fitted the child perfectly is an
elaborate creation which might have come
from a Paris dressmaker. The mother sits
down at her machine in the morning and
sews all day long, until she sews a stitch into
her back and a pain in her side and an ache
into her temples—until she is all demoral-
ized and feels ready to fly.

A good rule for the even-tempered wife is

not to attempt too much. A lady writing in *Harper's Bazar* not long ago, on "Temper or Nerves," gave an example of the way in which the mother loses control of herself. Her little story began thus :

"I wonder where temper ends and nerves begin?" said a weary mother whom I was visiting. She had just accused herself of being cross. I said she was nervous. Which was it?

"I am tired and intolerably cross," she insisted. "My temper is horrid, and yet I do try to control it. What is it?" as a knock came at the door.

"It's me, ma'am," and Bridget's red face appeared in the entrance. "Was it pease or beans you said you wanted for lunch?"

"Pease, Bridget. I ordered them from the grocer."

"Yes, ma'am. And when you was orderin' I forgot to say as there wasn't a taste of butter in the house."

"Oh, Bridget ! and now the man has gone with the order. I asked you particularly if you had everything for the day."

"Sure an' I forgot butter ! Oh, yes, and there ain't no salad-oil, and you'll want it with the lettuce at lunch."

The mistress said nothing for a moment, and then spoke with deadly calm :

"Since you forgot those things you will have to go to the grocer's to get them. But hurry, for you know this is a busy day."

"All right," sullenly.

As the sound of the heavy footsteps died on the stairs, the door of my hostess's room burst open and the ten-year-old son of the house rushed in.

"Mamma, where's my geography?"

"Just where you left it, my son."

"But I've forgotten, mamma! Oh dear, just see that clock! Five minutes to nine!"

"And you are ten minutes from school! My boy, why are you so careless? Look in the nursery for your book."

A scamper across the hall and then a triumphant shout from the nursery:

"Mamma, I've found it! Did I leave my hat in your room?"

"No, Harry."

"Where is it?"

"I don't know. You must find it, dear."

A deadly silence, during which I saw that the mother held herself still by main force. The hand with which she sewed quivered, the fingers closed tightly on the needle.

Then the clock struck nine.

"Mamma," wailed the boy, "it is nine o'clock, and I *can't* find my hat! What shall I do?"

And then the thread with which the mother sewed snapped, and something else—was it temper or nerves?—snapped too. Throwing down her work and springing from her chair she ran into the nursery, where, in the middle of the floor. she found the child's hat.

Putting it on his head and thrusting his books into his hand, she pushed him to the stair-head.

"You drive me wild by your heedlessness!" she exclaimed excitedly. "If you forget another thing to-day, I'll *whip* you!"

Then she returned to her room, sank into a chair, and buried her face in her hands.

"Oh, my wicked, wicked temper!" she moaned. "Women excuse this kind of thing as nervousness. I say it is temper, uncontrollable and sinful! And I am ashamed through and through!"

Which was it? And what is that with which many of us women fight daily as with an enemy to health and happiness? Shall we call it nervous irritability, or irritable nervousness?

Is it temper or nerves?

Just for example's sake we will suppose that that little boy on his way to school should be run over by a trolley car, or should meet with some sudden accident, or that that night he should be taken ill and go down to the door of death. How the mother would then reproach herself for the lack of patience she had shown!

In the light of Eternity many things will seem to us very trivial which now appear all important, and it will appear very strange to us that we could have allowed in ourselves such variations of mood when all that was needed was to hold closely and firmly the hand of Him who says, "As thy days thy strength shall be."

## OUR OWN.

If I had known in the morning
   How wearily all the day
      The words unkind
      Would trouble my mind
   I said when you went away,
I had been more careful, darling,
   Nor given you needless pain;
      But we vex "our own"
      With look and tone
   We might never take back again.

For though in the quiet evening
   You may give me the kiss of peace,
      Yet well it might be
      That never for me
   The pain of the heart should cease.
How many go forth in the morning
   Who never come home at night;
      And hearts have broken
      For harsh words spoken
   That sorrow can ne'er set right.

We have careful thought for the stranger,
   And smiles for the sometime guest,
      But oft for "our own"
      The bitter tone,
   Though we love our own the best.
Ah! lip with the curve impatient,
   Ah! brow with that look of scorn,
      'Twere a cruel fate
      Were the night too late
   To undo the work of the morn.

## To an English clergyman we are indebted

for the following admirable set of rules, for
everyday guidance.

1. Learn to govern yourselves, and to be
gentle and patient.

2. Guard your tempers, especially in seasons of ill-health, irritation, and trouble,
and soften them by prayers and a sense of
your own shortcomings and errors.

3. Never speak or act in anger until you
have prayed over your words or acts, and
concluded that Christ would have done so
in your place.

4. Remember that, valuable as is the gift
of speech, silence is often more valuable.

5. Do not expect too much from others,
but forbear and forgive, as you desire for-
bearance and forgiveness yourself.

6. Never retort a sharp or angry word.
It is the second word that makes the quarrel.

7. Beware of the first disagreement.

8. Learn to speak in a gentle tone of
voice.

9. Learn to say kind and pleasant things
whenever opportunity offers.

10. Study the character of each and sympathize with all in their troubles, however
small.

11. Do not neglect little things if they can
affect the comfort of others in the smallest
degree.

12. Avoid moods and pets and fits of
sulkiness.

13. Learn to deny yourself and prefer others.

14. Beware of meddlers and tale-bearers.

15. Never charge a bad motive if a good one is conceivable.

16. Be gentle and firm with children.

## SUNSHINY HUSBANDS.

From time immemorial it has been en-
joined upon wives to be bright and cheerful
in all circumstances.  They are told that
whether things have gone pleasantly or the
opposite in the household, whether they are
tired or not, no matter what burdens may
be put upon them, it is imperative that they
shall always speed their husbands away in
the morning with a cheerful face and meet
them on their return from business with a
bright smile and a pleasant word.

It seems to me that the duty of cheerfulness is quite as obligatory upon husbands
as upon wives, and that equally with women
men should rise above the petty trials and
irritations of the day and speak with agreeable consideration for others, lightening
the loads of life by the merry jest and the
happy manner.  Under the great stress of
calamity human nature girds itself to bear
whatever comes with fortitude.  None of
us is inadequate to meeting with fortitude
great disasters which sweep from us much
that has made life beautiful and dear, but
in the little vexations and disappointments
of every day we sometimes fall short of our
ideals.

4

The man who goes to business, to the
office, the shop, or the desk in the counting-
room, has the advantage over his wife that
he leaves his home behind him, enters upon
clearly defined duties for the day, in which
he is not liable to very much interruption,
and when night comes he simply turns the
key in his desk and goes home to find a
bright fire, children glad to see him, and a
supper table spread for his return.   Through
the day he has been meeting people in a
business way, and he has perhaps had business anxieties to bear, but only one set of
his faculties have been engaged and he may,
as it were, side-track the whole of that part
of his mind which has been occupied with
the worries of business, leave all cares behind him, and go home to something fresh
and pleasant.

His wife, on the contrary, has had a thousand little things to try her all day.   Should
the average man change places for one week
with his wife, engage in the multiform occupations which distract her—the mending, the
making, the contriving, the caring for babies,
tying up cut fingers, binding up burns and
bruises, conciliating Bridget or doing without Bridget altogether, preparing three meals
a day and clearing away the dishes when
they are over—he would realize the truth of
the old adage,

> " Man works from sun to sun,
> But woman's work is never done."

and he would understand far better than it
is possible to show him that the constant
iteration, the drop by drop, inch by inch
of woman's work in the house is what wears
her out.

I have seldom met a man who realized
that there was any need for the annual
house-cleaning which women know to be
imperative. A man invariably says, "Why
do you wish to stir things up ; everything
always looks clean. So it does to his inex-
perienced eyes. In fact, he never is there
when the furniture is pulled out of its place,
the carpet swept, and the administration of
broom and dusting-cloth and scrubbing-brush
are going on ; he goes away in the morning
before the work begins and comes back
when it is finished. In a sense this is somewhat different in the case of a farmer, whose
work lying often nearer his home enables
him to come in now and then through the
day. And yet in the case of a farmer's wife
the work is more strenuous than that required of any other woman in the same
station of life. She has, as a rule, fewer
things to do with, fewer labor-saving appli-
ances, and very often there are seasons of
the year when work presses in the fields and
her family is increased by the necessity of
boarding and lodging hired helpers of her
husband when it often happens that she can
get no domestics to assist her. The work
falls very heavily on farmers' wives and

daughters, and their bowed shoulders and weary looks tell the tale of life's burdens.

It is the greatest boon to a wife in any station when her husband has the habit of cheerfulness. When you see the children rushing with glad faces and merry shouts to welcome father's return at night, when the wife puts aside all her little worries, saying "When John comes home I will tell him everything," then you see one of the most beautiful sights on earth—a man cheerily bearing burdens.

Nothing is quite so sweet in this world as the tenderness of a strong man. Sometimes when we were travelling we have seen a big, gentle, kind man rise from his seat and take a fretful baby from the mother's arms, and very soon the little crying creature, rested and hushed, lays its little head against his broad breast and goes quietly asleep in those protecting arms.

A man who is loving, tender, and cheery is almost as good in this weary world as an angel from heaven. A lady once said to me:

" My sister and I are very differently placed in life, though we both have excellent husbands. Max, her husband, is of a very nervous temperament and of what we might call a difficult disposition to get on with, although he is a most honorable and excellent man. But Frances becomes perfectly worn out in the effort to have everything just as it always ought to be. The children are taught that they must behave well in the presence of their father. No matter what goes wrong Fanny carefully keeps it from Max, and we are all afraid now that she is on the brink of nervous prostration herself ; she has had so many small worries with nobody in the world to give her a lift in bearing them.

"With me the case is entirely different ; I fly to Jack with everything. The moment he comes into the house he brings in a great burst of sunshine. If one of the children is ill, it is he who takes the entire charge. If I am going away on a journey it is he who always packs my trunk. In fact, since the day I was married I have never had a single thing to do or to bear which my darling Jack could save me."

We cannot expect that every man will be able to emulate the example of Jack, but there is a measure of loving cheerfulness in the power of all men, and they can make their homes and their lives very beautiful if they will only put it into practice. I re-member once to have read a story by Rose Terry Cooke about a certain New England farmer who was what the people in his neighborhood called a street angel ; that is, he was charming to every one he met out-side his own front door, but when he came home he made up for this by being distress-ingly fault-finding to everybody within it.

There is one point on which husbands need to be very guarded and that is in the

matter of fault-finding at the table.   In fact,
there are three kinds of fault-finding which I
advise men of all ages to exorcise from their
lives as they would demons of destruction.
Never, dear John or Will, wherever you may
be, quote your mother's housekeeping at
your wife, never say "My mother always
did this or that," in a manner which reflects
discredit on your wife, the probabilities being that your wife's housekeeping is quite up
to the mark, and that it is only the glamour
of memory which casts so fair a sheen over
that of your mother.

Never, as you value domestic peace,
mention anything to the disadvantage of the
carving-knife.   I take it as a test of the most
thorough good breeding and amiability
when I never hear a man say "It passes
comprehension that our carving-knife is
always so dull.   What in the world do you
do with it ?   Is it used to cut the bread, or to
hack the soles off the children's shoes ?   I
am sure if this carving-knife were kept in
the right way and used only on the table
there would be nothing the matter with it."
The demon of perversity which lurks around
carving-knives has a fearful effect on the
tempers of the most lovely and ordinarily
urbane men.

Also do not find fault with the food itself.
It is quite as much to your wife's interest to
have her table nicely appointed and her food
well cooked as it is to yours, and should

an accident ever happen and something be
heavy which ought to be light, or burned
which should have been underdone, she is
as grieved and sorry and ashamed in the
matter as you can possibly be.

I was once a guest for some time in the
home of one of the truest gentlemen I have
ever known.   One day there came upon the
table a roast which was fabulously tough.
The wife, who was the caterer and pur-
veyor, as wives usually are, felt very much
distressed, but her husband said, "Why,
Maggie, you are not responsible for this,
you did the very best you could ; no one
could have done any better.   And in this
town we are so dependent on the boats which
bring us supplies and it is so hard to market
that I am constantly astonished that our
table is so beautifully kept."    That was the
way in which to meet such a contretemps.

No right-minded or sunshiny husband will
ever find fault with anything which goes on
underneath his roof if he can help it.   If his
buttons happen to be off he will realize that
the omission was not intentional, and in
every possible way he will make the best of
things.   In doing so he will teach his boys
to do the same.   Boys and young men catch
their father's tone toward the women of the
household, and where you find a husband
uniformly courteous, uniformly gentle of
speech and sweet of manner, you find boys
growing up after the same pattern.

Let me say in addition to this that no class of people seem to me so really noble at the core and so self-denying as American husbands. They are contented to work year in and year out for the advancement and pleasure of their families. Nothing is too hard for them. They ask little for themselves. They are proud of their wives and daughters, and their faults, such as they are, are usually on the surface and do not go very deeply. But one may neutralize the effect of a thousand real sacrifices by a disagreeable manner, and many a good man is not appreciated as he should be because he has not learned to control the expression of disapproval or the little action in his own home which would be impossible to him in that of a stranger.

Patience, no matter what is our appointed lot, is a wise prescription for us all to take. Let us remember that

" One stitch and another stitch, and the longest rent is mended ;
One step and another step, and the longest way is ended."

It will not be very long before for all of us the way will be ended, and nothing can be more delightful than to be remembered as always having made the best of things, always having been sweet and courageous and pure and a blessing to all whom we have met. On a little grave in

Vermont there stands a stone with this inscription :

## OUR MOTHER.

*She was always so pleasant.*

Why should not fathers, equally with mothers, earn this description ?

## PARENTS AND CHILDREN.

The inexperience of childhood, its dependence and its helplessness in the hands of
those who have it in charge should make
us who are older think very seriously on
the subject of children's rights.  In these
days what is called "child culture" has become a fad, and many people are studying
children, their habits and little ways, trying
to discover their points of view, and acting
very much as botanists do when they an-
alyze a plant.

After all, the great requirements for children are sympathy and freedom.  The parent must try to put himself or herself in the
child's place, must remember that a little
being who has been only a few years in the
world cannot judge of things as older people do, and must give the child a chance to
develop naturally along its own lines.

This is not to say that children should
not be taught obedience and truthfulness.
It is a child's right to learn that in this world
all things move according to law, and the
kind father and mother try to show the child
from the very first that all happiness con-
sists in harmony, that the disagreeable, fret-

ful and unreasonable child makes a jar and
discord which was not intended by God,
and that, not because of the parents' will,
but in order that the child may learn self-
control, the older must lead the younger in
paths of righteousness.

Dr. John Brown of Edinburgh remarks in
an essay entitled "My Father's Memoir,"
"My first recollection of my father, my first
impression, not only of his character, but
of his eyes and face and presence, strange
as it may seem, dates from my fifth year.
Doubtless I had looked at him often enough
before that, and had my own childish
thoughts about him; but this was the time
when I got my fixed, compact idea of him,
and the first look of him which I felt could
never be forgotten. I saw him, as it were,
by a flash of lightning, sudden and complete.

"A child begins by seeing bits of everything; it knows in part—here a little, there
a little; it makes up its wholes out of its
own littles, and is long in reaching the fulness of a whole; and in this we are children
all our lives, in much. Children are long of
seeing, or at least of looking at what is above
them; they like the ground, and its flowers
and stones, its 'red-sodgers' and lady-birds,
and all its queer things; their world is about
three feet high, and they are more often
stooping than gazing up. I know I was
past ten before I saw, or cared to see, the

ceilings of the rooms in the manse at Biggar."

I think we forget very often how limited is the world of childhood. Very few grown people remember just what their aims and dreams and pleasures and feelings were when they were little creatures in the nursery or during the first years of school life. Many times it appeared to them as if the grown people around them, parents and teachers, were arbitrary beings, invested with power which they used with little thought of the children's convenience and pleasure.

Children are being constantly interrupted. No matter what they are doing—building houses of blocks, drawing pictures on their slates, reading an interesting story—it is expected that they will at once drop every pursuit of their own, and go pleasantly and even eagerly on the errands of their elders.

That little feet should run on other people's errands and little hands should always be ready to be obliging is so true and so necessary, not only to their own culture, but to the machinery of our homes, in order that all may run smoothly, that we sometimes forget to be considerate where our juniors are concerned.

I hold that one should not needlessly interrupt a child in its occupations, that every favor asked of one younger than ourselves should be a matter of politeness, that we

should say "Please" and "I beg pardon"
to the little ones, that we should thank
them for what they do for us precisely as
we apologize and acknowledge and are
courteous to our older friends.

There is a sweet atmosphere about some
homes, an atmosphere of kind feeling, confidence and good-will, and it is usually discovered that this reigns where parents are
polite to children, and where children are
trained by example as well as by precept in
the practice of gentle speech and of an
obliging, accommodating disposition.

We have no right to force upon children
food which is disagreeable to their palates.
Of course there is such a thing as a capricious child who rejects what is good for him
and changes his mind several times in an
hour. When such a child is found we may
be sure that back of him stands a foolish
and capricious mother, who has had so little
common sense in her management that she
has fostered in the child these disagreeable
ways.

A few days ago, at a summer hotel, I witnessed an exhibition of ill-temper on the
part of a mother toward a little child, at a
public table, which shocked not only myself but the others in the company. One
lady said almost audibly, "That mother is
going to make of her child a liar and a
coward." Another, a physician of distinction, said, "I was sorely tempted to inter-

fere and say to the mother that she forgot that the nervous impressionability of children is very great, and that such scenes would be remembered by her little one in years to come."

The child tried to explain something to his mother, but every time he said, "Mamma, please let me tell you," the mother said, very sternly, "Hush this instant ; if you say another word I will send you to bed without your supper. I don't wish to hear anything about it." And thus she went on, speaking in loud, impatient tones, forgetful of the fact that she was making of herself an exhibition of weakness most pitiful to behold.

If we would have gentle, well-bred children, we must treat them with gentleness and consideration ourselves. Miss Lillie Hamilton French, writing in *Harper's Bazar*, thus sums up one side of the matter when she speaks of The Spirit of the Eternal Don't.

"It may belong to one of the great dual forces that rule life—belong, in other words, to the negative as distinguished from the positive forces, and be therefore rightly accounted for in the general ordering of the universe. And yet, when all is said and done, it must certainly be confessed that few things are capable of making life so unpleasant and so disastrous as this spirit once rampant among our friends.

"Some persons are altogether controlled

both in thought and action by it. They stand as eternal protests against whatever is or whatever is about to be. They contribute nothing and oppose all things. They set up their petty prejudice or personal predilection, and expect to damn with them the incoming currents of renewing life.

" 'What is your name?' asked some one of a small boy who was always being nagged. 'Charley Don't,' he answered, having in his cheerful imperturbability mistaken the invariable accompaniment to his Christian name.

"But few of us have the imperturbability of this child under the don'ts of our families or our friends. Some of us have our spontaneity crushed. Some of us grow rebellious and indignant, and are in this way forced into opposite extremes, getting off our balance on the other side. And most of us grow self-conscious, and have periods in which we question every one of our best impulses, weighing them against our motives.

"The development of many young persons sensitive to impressions is retarded for years by the thoughtless don't of an elder whose opinions they have been taught to respect. For many of the don'ts are thoughtless, springing from habit, and not from serious consideration. I know a wise old lady who said don't so many times one morning to a grown-up daughter that she detected herself in it at last and laughed. 'Don't pay any attention to me,' she said at last, 'I only say it, because I always have.'

"Circumstances present us with so many impediments, one often wonders why our fellow-men should want to provide us with so many more; why they should perpetually say, for instance, 'Oh, don't do that!' when we happen to make a courteous remark to some one they do not know, or when we have a hospitable instinct they do not share, or a charitable impulse they do not on the instant share. For the curious part of all is this—when the rewards of our best impulses (those opposed by them) are reaped, they settle complacently down to take a smiling share in them. How proudly parents bask in the sunshine of a child's success whose new departure they once thwarted with all their strength and authority! And the reverse of this is true—how we are condemned for losing that which the don'ts of another have driven out of us. Some law of right is at work with us, and the penalty all pay for having interfered with another's development is that we live to mourn the loss of that which we have suppressed. We repulse with a don't the demonstrations of our children and of those who are nearest to us, and we live to perish of hunger for them.

"The spirit of the don't rules in the Ten Commandments; but when the higher dis-

pensation, came in the Beatitudes given on
another Mount, it was no longer 'Thou
shalt *not,*' but 'Blessed *are.*'

"How many of us who try to rule others
with don'ts are capable of suggesting even
what a substitute for the thing proscribed
ought to be? We say don't to a child who
offends us by loud speech, but can we show
him the right tones instead? Can we teach
him to pitch his voice in a lower key, or
will we even be at pains to do it?

Another right of children on which, in
view of their relations to the world at large
as well as to their parents, we cannot too
much insist, is on their being believed whatever they may say. We teach children
to be untruthful by doubting their word.
Children live in a sort of imaginative world.
They often make extraordinary statements
simply because they are romancing in the
fairyland in which they live, but they do
not mean to be in the least untrue. The
thing for us to do is to accept their statements, and when they become too poetical
to gradually lead the child back to the
prosaic land in which we live. Heaven
lies about us in our infancy, and

"Trailing clouds of glory do we come
From Heaven, which is our home."

It does not take many years to dispel the
starry haze, luminous, yet vague, in which

5

we walk at first. Before long, as children grow older, they learn to discriminate between the ideal and the real. If we invariably speak the truth to them ; if we keep our promises to the very letter, whether or not it is convenient for us to do so ; if we use as few threats as possible, but carry them out relentlessly ; if, in short, our children live in a world of perfect truth and sincerity, they will be true themselves. Never let a child know, if you can help it, that there is such a thing as a lie in the world.

If you wish lovely, agreeable and delightful children, of whom you can be proud before your friends, and who will do the family credit wherever they go, be sure that they live in a home atmosphere full of sunshine, that their rate of health is kept at the highest, and from an early age they learn that they are not their own, but are, like all the rest of us, responsible for their deeds to the Heavenly Father.

Dr. Holland, in his Letters to the Joneses, has some very sensible words to over-anxious parents, those who govern as the czar does by an absolute despotism, wholly exacted from the outside. After talking very plainly to one of the conscientious, but everlastingly nagging sort of mothers who *do* exist, to the crushing of all joy in childhood, and the effacing of individual traits in young people, this judicious counsellor says pithily :

"You ask me what I really mean by all this, for you are a practical woman, and are not to be taken in by a set of easily written phrases. Well, I will try to explain, or illustrate, my meaning. I remember a gathering at your house—a party of friends—to which your children were admitted; and I remember with painful distinctness the telegraphic communication which you maintained with them during the whole evening. If James got his legs crossed, or, in his drowsiness, gaped, or if he coughed, or sneezed, or laughed above a certain key, or made a remark, or moved his chair, it was: 'James, h—m!'—'James, h—m!' 'James, h—m!' And James was only one of half a dozen whom you treated in the same way. You began the evening with the feeling that you were entirely responsible for the behavior of those children —just as much responsible as if they severally were the fingers of your hand. You acted as if they were machines which, for the evening, you had undertaken to operate. They felt that they were under the eye of a vigilant keeper, and they did not dream of such a thing as acting for themselves. They were acting for you, and they did not know until they heard your suggestive 'h—m!' whether they were right or wrong. You undertook for the evening to be to them in the stead of their sense of propriety; and the communication between them and you

being imperfect, they often offended. I
know that your own good sense will tell
you now that this is not the way gentlemen
and ladies are made.

" I was recently in a family circle where I
witnessed a most delightful contrast to all
this—where the sons and daughters were
brought up and introduced to me by the
father and mother with as much politeness
and cordiality as if they were kings and
queens every one, and with as much freedom as if the parents had not the slightest
doubt that the children—from the oldest to
the youngest—would bear themselves like
ladies and gentlemen.  There was no for-
wardness on the part of these children, as
you may possibly suppose ; yet there was
perfect self-possession ; and each child knew
that he stood upon his own merits.

"There was a feature of your family gov-
ernment (which you held in common with
your husband) that made still more complete the slavery of your children.  It was
the deacon's opinion, you will remember,
that a boy who was not too tired to play at
ball, or slide down hill, or skate, was not
too tired to saw wood, and it was his policy
to direct all the excess of animal life which
his boys manifested into the channels of in-
dustry and usefulness.  You seconded this
opinion, and maintained that a girl who was
not too sleepy to make a doll's hat, or a
doll's dress, was not too sleepy to hem a

handkerchief, or darn a stocking. So your children never had what children call 'a good time.' Always kept at work when possible, and always restrained in every exhibition of the spirit of play, home became an irksome place to them, and childhood a dreary period. Your children were never permitted to do anything to please themselves in their own way. Everything was done—or you insisted that everything should be done—to please you in your way. If one of your daughters sat down to rest, or resorted to a little quiet amusement, you stirred her at once by some petty command. I was often tempted to be angry with you because you would never give your children any peace. You had always something for them to do, and something that had to be done just at the very time when they were enjoying themselves the best.

"'Precept upon precept' is very well in its way, but principle is much better. The principle of right and proper acting, fully inculcated, renders unnecessary all precepts; and until a child has fully received this principle he is without the basis of manhood. The earlier this principle is received and a child thrown upon his own responsibility, and made to feel that he is a man, lacking only years to give him strength and wisdom, the safer that boy is for time and for eternity. The moment a boy becomes morally responsible, he becomes, in an important sense, free." There is pleasure and satisfaction in freedom, but only restraint and a continual sense of grievance, where slavery is maintained in the family.

## OVER-SENSITIVE PEOPLE.

A great deal of unhappiness results in this world from the quickness of people to take offence when none is intended. There are men who are forever going around with a chip on their shoulders, begging some one to knock it off. There are women who constantly wear an air of martyrdom; their feelings are so easily hurt that to live with them is like a perpetual walking on thin ice —you never know when you are going to break through. Such living is a strain on both parties, the offended and the offenders alike.

One of the faults against which we should guard ourselves is this facility of resentment; the fancying that people intend to wound us, when in fact nothing is further from their thoughts. We have all known people with whom it was never safe to talk of certain subjects; they acted upon them as the traditional red rag upon the bull in the pasture. Others—and these not infrequently the ones most ready to jest themselves—are exceedingly annoyed if any one makes fun, even in the most good-humored way, of anything they do. They cannot have liber-

ties taken with them, and woe to him or her
who dares to invade their conscious dignity.

Such people are not pleasant to live with,
nor do they usually make many friends.
Why should we not take it for granted that
those with whom we associate are, as a rule,
kind-hearted and good-natured, and that
they intend nothing but good when they are
talking with us?

I will, however, let a caution come in
against one person who is to be avoided as
a plague and a bore wherever he is found.
One can hardly be over-sensitive in speaking of this individual, who goes about enjoying himself at the expense of his friends, and
whose conduct is worthy the greatest repro-
bation,—I mean the person who engages in
the practical jest.

A practical jest is seldom permissible, and
it often has very bad and long-continued
results. I have myself known of cases in
which a fatal shock was given to one who
was frightened by seeing some one step out
of the dark wrapped in a sheet, or by the
presence of a pretended burglar in the room,
or by some other foolishness, which, after
all, had a droll side only to the one who
originated it. The practical jest has not a
single aspect which is even tolerable.

Apart from practical jesting, the harmless
fun and drollery of life are to be cultivated,
and they are very unwise who allow themselves to be disturbed because the people

around them choose to say witty or humorous things even at their expense. Join in the laugh, and refuse to consider your *amour-propre*.

A good plan is sometimes to tell a story against one's self ; and do not refuse to be genuinely amused if somebody else tells a good story of which you are the theme.

People are apt to say in anger things which they express more strongly than they would if they waited for a moment of calmness. Impulsive natures often go too far, and use exaggeration when modified statements would be truer. In all questions of domestic discussion and in committee meetings and churches, and wherever people gather socially, differences of opinion will arise, and there will always be some who say a little more than they mean, or some who preserve a silence which is in itself a reproof or a reproach.

Instead of carrying away a heartache or even a transient pain from such encounters, the wiser way is to discount in one's mind that which has been said in haste, and to await the cool leisure of after-thought before making any rejoinder. A sensible woman once said, "It never occurs to me as at all possible that anybody would like to hurt my feelings, or that anybody could snub me." In consequence, this dear lady walked tranquilly through life, never taking offence, always happy and pleased.

Intense self-consciousness is at the bottom
of most of our touchiness. Can you fancy
Queen Victoria ever feeling that anybody
wishes to pass her by with neglect? And
shall not each of us in her place consider
herself quite as much a Queen as the splendid woman who has so long sat upon England's throne?

In a very lovely book which I suppose
almost everybody has read, "Cranford,"
there is given a charming instance of a man
who was popular, partly because positively
oblivious of anything intended to so much
as criticise his ordinary behavior. Cranford
was a little place inhabited mainly by
women—widows and spinsters—living on
small incomes. Life moved in Cranford
with great quietude and little friction.
Everybody knew what everybody else had
to spend and felt called upon to put the
best foot foremost on all occasions, always,
however, with entire politeness and consideration for others.

To this little town of Cranford came
Captain Brown and his two daughters, Jessie
and Mary. To have a man living in the
place at all, and constantly around, as a re-
tired officer without occupation had occasion
to be, was at first considered rather an inflic-
tion by the ladies of the place. They did
not know how they would get along with
Captain Brown; and, indeed, the Captain's
unaffected, manly ways of doing things,

his loud voice, his large feet, his hearty way of laughing and shouting around the place troubled and disturbed the dear ladies very much.

But they presently found that it did no good to turn cold looks and faces upon Captain Brown. He was entirely unaware of giving them any displeasure. Presently it was discovered that the new element was not at all objectionable, and that Captain Brown's ready and gentle hand in passing a teacup, his constant patience with his invalid daughter, his chivalry to pretty Miss Jessie, and his general air of good fellowship with all the world, made Cranford much more entertaining than it had formerly been.

When one does not seem to feel darts and arrows ; when these simply glance against an armor of reserve and indifference, the persons who throw them soon cease to find amusement in the occupation. Perhaps it would be well for some of us to learn the stolidity of other races than ours ; the Chinaman, for instance, and the Indian are trained from the cradle to show no emotion whatever, either of pleasure or pain, and their faces are masks behind which no one knows what may be going on. To some extent this stolidity is to be desired as a shield against needless wounding and pain.

If we wear our heart on our faces, our

faces grow old faster. Still, one would not like to see a number of immobile, expressionless people going about; life would then be colorless and stagnant. Can we not draw the line at allowing our faces to show only feelings of pleasure and goodwill, keeping from them exasperation, indignation, hatred, contempt, and all the malevolent emotions, and permitting them to reveal only the sweet, gentle, and beautiful thoughts which come and go in our minds? Beware, too, of being too literal, too intensely matter-of-fact. Cultivate imagination as a healing balm for many stings.

After all, we may as well be as happy as we can in this world. Enough trouble will come to us which we cannot possibly ward away. It is always within our power to defend ourselves from those wounds which are simply made in our self-love. Vanity is a plant of very strong growth, striking its roots deep down into the soil of human nature. If we could be entirely free from vanity, it is doubtful whether it would occur to us to be hurt or over-sensitive, and to take offence when no offence is intended.

Mrs. Alice Hamilton Rich, in a thoughtful paper, says:

"How often we hear the expression, 'I am so sensitive,' when, if the truth were told, it would be, 'I am so selfish.' By sensitiveness is usually meant more than usual refinement. This may be true if we substitute refinement of selfishness, or inordinate self-consciousness. More often it is the woman, still oftener the young girl, who prides herself on her sensitiveness. If it is the little child, the foolish mother speaks of this quality as something of which to be proud, and because of which her child at home, in school, in society, ought to receive special consideration. This is either given or not given, as teacher or friends see fit. If it is given, the child grows more selfish. Friends still politely call it sensitiveness as years are added to the young life. If mothers could but realize what obstacles to success and happiness they are themselves placing before their children, they would help their children to be sensible and unselfish, the two qualities which will, if planted early and closely to the sensitive plant, choke out the weed, for it is a weed.

"While selfishness is at the root of sensitiveness, self-consciousness is often the immediate cause. The one who most fully forgets self is least likely to see reason to be sensitive. It is really an inordinate appreciation of self which makes one live in the look-out tower and invite the shafts of the enemy and bare his bosom to the smiter. If a woman busies herself in home, church, or philanthropic work ; if a man, when not occupied with business duties, interests himself in his own children and becomes absorbed in some recreative

study, there will be little time to give thought
to unpleasant criticisms, still less for the
imaginary slights of neighbors and friends."
A real gentleman and lady are unconscious of
self, and hence perfectly at ease.   The true
man and woman are unselfishly desirous to
be helpful to others.   Not that they may
receive their own with usury, but because
the heart of the giver is overflowing with a
wealth of blessed helpfulness which must
find objects and places for its expression
and overflow.

"The so-called sensitive woman unites
with the church, either taking upon herself
the duties of membership for the first time
or coming from a sister church.   Usually
such an one is pleased with the immediate
welcome accorded to her.   In a general
way she is invited to the meetings of the
church.   Very soon some members of the
various women's societies ask her to join
them.   Perhaps she comes once or twice
and is cordially welcomed.   Only a few of
the busy workers find time to call upon her.
She is sensitive, thinks she is not properly
looked after, ceases to put herself in the
way of the working women,  making no
place for herself in the church work, remains at home, and is soon really and truly
forgotten.

"Whose fault is it?   No doubt partially
that of the older members, but more truly
her own.   She was given an opportunity to

become acquainted with her sisters in the church and to make herself a power, if not an aggressive element, in church work. But, as she says, she was too sensitive to push herself where she was not wanted. Most likely her sensitiveness was pure self-ishness and an exaggerated estimate of her own value. She was wanted. There was a place waiting for her, as for any one who earnestly seeks after it, but busy women have no time to run after those who will not meet them half way. The woman who is so sensitive, that she needs coaxing, is too sensitive for any use. She may as well step aside into her small corner to brood, at her own sweet will, over fancied slights, while the women who put themselves into the working circle widen and broaden their in-fluence as the circle grows larger and larger, until the influence which they exert is truly marvellous.

"One often hears women say, 'I cannot become an officer in a society or a promi-nent member of a committee, I am so sensi-tive about what others say of me.'

"Which is the more important, the needed work or the possible criticism of the worker? Is it sensitiveness or a selfish putting of one's own ease and comfort paramount to the good which needs to be done? If in the judgment of wise women one is suited for a special work, why not accept the work, do one's best, and take no anxious thought

of what 'they say.' Very likely mistakes
will be made, criticisms be given ; but why
should you and I keep ourselves apart from
the workers lest we be so unfortunate as to
make mistakes or be misunderstood ? After
all, each one of us as individuals are of little
consequence save to ourselves and immediate friends, and doubtless less is said of
us than we in our egotism think."

## SINGING IN THE RAIN.

Hear my happy little bird
    Singing through the rain—
Singing while the fitful showers
    Dash against the pane.
"Blue sky somewhere," carols he,
    From his fearless heart,
Though the clouds are gathering thick,
    And the chill winds start.

Sweet and shrill the silver notes
    Weave a wordless strain ;
"Blue sky somewhere," in my thought
    Is their glad refrain.
Always sunshine just beyond,
    Brief the present ill,
Trouble never long to last,
    Is their meaning still.

Sing thy sweetest, merry bird,
    Comforter of mine,
Bringing, in thy little way,
    Help from Love divine ;
Thou hast given me the clasp
    Of a golden chain,
Let from heaven into my hand,
    Through the clouds and rain

What though all my way be hedged,
   Love shall ope a door
For the feet that follow fain
   His that went before.
What though trials test my faith,
   Peace shall yet maintain
Right to rule in one who walks
   Singing in the rain.

More than I can count of good
   Aye has been my share;
Dearest hands to help me on,
   Having all my care;
Blessings marking every way,
   To the latest one,
And the shadow only proof
   Of the glowing sun

Therefore, with undaunted front,
   Trusting in my King,
Shall I face whatever foe
   In the path may spring.
So I hear a note of cheer
   In the brave refrain
Of my merry little bird,
   Singing in the rain.

6

## THE CHILD'S POINT OF VIEW.

One of the most interesting families of
whom I have ever heard was that wonderful Quaker family named Gurney who lived
in Earlham, England, just about one hundred years ago.  The family of the Gurneys
was very simple and rural.  There were
four sons and seven daughters, all of whom
were brought up in habits of great affection
and loyalty by an excellent mother, part of
whose creed was that a woman's life ought
to be passed in regulating the affairs of her
family.

In a memorandum found after Mrs. Gurney's death, she says that "A wife should
work plain work neatly herself, and understand the cutting-out of linen ; also, she
should not be ignorant of the common pro-
prieties of the table, or deficient in the
economy of any of the most minute affairs
of a family.  It should be here observed
that gentleness of manner is indispensably
necessary in women, to say nothing of that
polished behavior which adds a charm to
every qualification ; and to both of these it
appears certain that children may be led,

without vanity or affectation, by amiable and judicious instruction."

Of the children of this Gurney family several came to great estate, and all were very useful in their day and generation. Samuel Gurney became a great banker and philanthropist, a man universally respected and beloved. In his old age a silversmith in Norwich was suspected of having committed forgery, which in those days was punishable with death. Mr. Gurney investigated the case, and, being convinced of the man's entire innocence, himself went and stood beside him in the prisoner's dock, a sight which so impressed all beholders that the question of the man's acquittal was very soon settled.

Joseph Gurney was equally well-known for integrity and clinging to what he thought was right. Elizabeth, spoken of in the family during childhood as Betsey, became the celebrated Mrs. Elizabeth Fry, who was to the convicts and criminals of her day the benefactor and friend which Mrs. Ballington Booth is endeavoring to be to the unfortunate prisoners of our own period. Indeed, it is hard to find anywhere a family so extraordinary, and so distinguished for their goodness and freedom from ambition, as these Quaker Gurneys of Earlham.

The mother died when the youngest of her eleven children was a baby and the oldest a young girl. Upon the shoulders of

Catherine Gurney, before she was twenty, came the care and mothering of the great brood of brothers and sisters; and she filled the place of mother and sister wonderfully, with rare discretion, tact, and loving self-forgetfulness.

As few families have ever more worthily filled a place in their generation, and as they were noted for good-breeding and good manners as well as for principle, I think it pertinent to the subject to introduce a rather prolonged mention of them here. In the first place, we will take a peep at the journal kept by a little girl, Louisa Gurney, one hundred years ago. Reading between the lines, we shall see how this child was trained in the eternal verities and also in the little conventionalities which make life happy or miserable, as they are practised or neglected.

"April 3, 1796.—I am eleven years old. I love my father better than anybody except Kitty; she is everything to me. I cannot feel that she has a fault, and I am sure that I shall always continue to love her as I do now. To dear Rachel I feel differently. I should love her more if I thought she loved me half as much as I love her. To Betsy I feel a particular sort of attachment; her ill-health and sweetness draw my heart to her entirely. John I love very much. To Chenda, how odd I feel! I often long to be intimate with her, but can't; I am so

sharply repulsed. I think Hannah a superior girl in many respects, but she has some
disagreeable qualities. I love the three dear
little boys heartily : they will be charming
men. I love dearest Elizabeth truly, and
am more intimate with her than with anybody in the world. I like all the Enfields
very much : I think they are a most delightful family.

"April 8.—I have done nothing to-day to
please anybody, nor the least good. I am
really a most disagreeable common character, and the reason why people love me can
be only from habit.

"April 15.—Kitty and Joseph and Dan
went to Cousin Freshfield's. We are never so
comfortable when Kitty is away. I am
always afraid of doing anything behind her
back that I would not do before her, and it
is difficult to be steadfast to what we know
she would like when she is not constantly
with us.

"June 1.—I will write about Earlham.
My father is master, Kitty is mistress. Governess, disliked by most of the family, sits in
the drawing-room almost all day. Rachel
and Betsy have their own employments.
Rachel and Kitty sleep together in the Blue
Room : the closet is entirely Rachel's. The
nursery is where Betsy, Hannah, Cilla, and
I sleep. The night-nursery is the boys'
room and nurse's. Chenda sleeps with the
governess. The first maid is Judd, a con-

vinced Friend and trustworthy old servant.
Nurse Sarah Williams comes next, and is
very particular about us : her greatest happiness is to see us neat ; she often tires me
by scoldings about keeping my clothes
neat. . . . Scarnell is a worthy man,
who has had the greatest concern to be a
Friend, and is now going to be one. Mr.
and Mrs. Driver and their baby live at the
lodge gate. . . . We have lived in this
sweet place ten years.

"June 13.—In the afternoon we walked
about instead of lessons—I do so like my
liberty. I think it most silly to bring children up to be always at work. I am sure I
should be better and happier if I did not
learn much ; it does try my temper so
much.

"June 21.—To-day is the great day of the
Yearly Meeting. All Friends come that
like it. We had not so many as usual, only
twenty-seven. We went to a long *dis*
(stands for disagreeable) meeting after breakfast.

"Rachel has begun to teach us our lessons.
I like her teaching very much, though not
nearly so much as Kitty's; she treats me
as other girls are treated, but Kitty treats us
as if we were reasonable creatures. I hate
the common way of teaching children ; people treat them as if they were idiots, and
never let them judge for themselves.

"July 31.—After breakfast I picked most

of the servants some gooseberries, and Judd's mother a whole basketful. How very good of me! I have the greatest pleasure in doing things to please others ; it is one of my best qualities.  .  .  .  Another of my qualities which people call most bad, but which I think rather good, is that I cannot bear strict authority over me. I do from the bottom of my heart *hate* the preference shown in all things to my elders merely because they have been in the world a little longer. I do love equality and true democracy.

"August 1.—I got up early and wrote to Elizabeth, who is rather *dis.* to me now. I do not like her as much as I did. I felt extremely cross in the morning, so many little things came to cross me. I have been quite struck lately with my own disagreeableness. We four did something in the afternoon which Kitty had forbidden us, and my conscience pinched me the whole time. I have also been rather selfish to-day.

"August 6.—Rachel sang in the evening. Kitty stood by me in the window. She took my hand and almost said she loved me. How charming ! All my old feelings of love to her returned. The evening was so delightful and Rachel's singing so touching ! I went to bed in the most happy frame of mind and body.

"August 10.—Betsy has talked to me, and quite convinced me that we do not treat my

father with sufficient love : but I really do
love my father from the bottom of my
heart.

August 19.—I was very angry with Rachel
for treating Chenda differently, just because
she is a little older than me ; there is nothing on earth I detest so much as this. I
think children ought to be treated according
to their merit, not their age. I love democracy, whenever and in whatever form it
appears.

"August 24.—I got up early and made a
pincushion for nurse's sister. I think it is
quite right to pay these sort of attentions to
servants, and if we do it out of kindness, it
is more virtue to give a present to a person
who has been rather ungrateful to you. I
hate Betsy's management of our lessons.
Now that Kitty is away at Northrepps, Betsy
does it, and is quite disagreeable, she is so
soon worried.

"Feb. 24, 1797.—I shall relate what has
passed in my mind lately. I think that I am
improved altogether. I have been extremely
busy, and have got into a good way of gaining knowledge, but I think I have grown
rather vain, which is a most disgusting fault.
Rachel has done me the greatest good. I
admire and love her more than I can say.
Being parted from dearest Kitty for some
time has not the least abated my love, but
it has encreased my fear of her. I do not
feel in the least intimate with her. which

often vexes me. She now and then takes us up, and does not allow us to have any opinion. These things would not be observed in any one else, but she is usually so kind, so good, and so charming, that even a cool word seems odd in her. And her present plan of treating us as children rather hurts me, being of a somewhat forward disposition. Pitchford has been here twice since Kitty has been gone, and we have had most delightful days. He brought us four a box of Portugal plums. I never knew anything so kind. We had a most charming walk in the afternoon, when we all quarrelled for Pitchford's arm ; we are so perfectly free with him. I can't say how I admire him. After dinner we talked very pleasantly till tea ; after that we acted pantomimes, and then read poetry and enjoyed ourselves thoroughly After supper was the most delightful time of any ; I did feel so happy. They sang ' Come, ye lads and lassies fair.'

"My father has been to dine with the Prince ; he likes him very much, and is delighted that he is coming here on seventh-day week. Uncle Joseph, and Hannah, and Jane have been here, and Uncle Joseph spoke to Rachel about going out to dances. He took her into the study, and when he was gone she burst out crying. I did pity her so much. I am afraid she must give it up. All our hope is now laid upon her having a pianoforte at home. They are trying this grand point

with my father : may they succeed, but I
much doubt it.

"April 26.—I always get up at five or six,
which I call late.   I read till breakfast, which
I enjoy amazingly ; the breakfast is a little
after eight.   I am most busy all the morning at lessons.   I have about an hour for
play.   We dine at three.   In the afternoon
I write my French exercise and journal, and
study botany, which I think is a most
charming employment ; to study nature in
any way is delightful.   We drink tea about
six, and have the most pleasant evenings.
We all sit and work while Kitty reads to us.
We have been reading Hayley's 'Triumph
of Temper,' which I only like tolerably.   I
went to Keswick yesterday.   Elizabeth and
I had a large syllabub, and sucked it through
straws.   I think my mind has been in a
very good state.   I am improving.   It is
very pleasant to think so sometimes.   One
of my chief faults is speaking unkindly to
Betsy : she does so provoke me.   She behaves in some things so aristocratically because she is the eldest, and nothing makes
me so angry as that.   How very pleasant is
Pitchford's company !   We had a charming
walk, and then we came in and sat round
the fire with Pitchford.   We talked most in-
terestingly, principally about religion.   I
can't say how much I admire what he said
—the happiness he had in prayer, and he
showed what a *most* delightful thing real de-

votion is, and what a comfort and support religion is to the mind. He spoke so charmingly and became so animated about it, it was enough to make one religious. I am determined I will be religious—*really* so, I mean. When Pitchford was gone, I went to bed, and lay awake till Kitty came. What Pitchford had said had gone so completely into my mind, that I thought about it the whole time, and somehow Kitty and I fell into talk about it. She said that it was only very lately that she had felt *real* devotion, and that it had made her far happier. I now intend to make it my aim to follow Pitchford and Kitty ; I never saw such perfect characters as they. The last time I was at Keswick, Elizabeth told me she wondered we were not all more charming than we are, living with Kitty. It rather hurt me : I don't know why, but it did. I believe it was because I felt it was true. I am determined I will try to make myself worthy of the pains that such a person as Kitty takes with me.

"I really see and know my own faults. I know that I have a great many, and that it will require time and patience to cure them. I do not think I have a bad temper, but, on the contrary, very good. I am very affectionate, and my heart is open to warm impressions. I can't bear restraint, and it is difficult to govern me by strictness, though very possible to do it by kindness and persuasion. I think I am not selfish, but the

contrary. I oppose all restraint with too
much vigor. I always tell my opinions and
think them better than those of other people
who are wiser than I am. I think I am
self-conceited. I have no mildness in my
character, for I only see the virtues of a few,
and look down with contempt upon the
general run. I am wanting in real fortitude,
though nothing is so useful.

"Oct. 13.—I have been in a good mind all
day. The others have been truly disagreeable and idle. I was much inclined to catch
the contagion, but I *would* not. I gave my
mind entirely to my lessons. How far better it is to give our minds to the things we
are about; it is the only way to do them
well."

This is taken from "The Gurneys of Earlham" by
Augustus Hare.

## THE SOCIAL RELATIONS OF BOYS AND GIRLS.

We make a mistake when by our arbitrary legislation we set boys and girls apart as if they were bound in association to do one another harm. God sets them in families where they are mutually helpful. In our blundering management we so contrive that it is from an early age almost impossible for young people between the periods of seven and sixteen years to meet in a perfectly natural and innocent manner on the common ground God gives them. When the children are still in kilts and frilled petticoats, we allow foolish people to put into their heads silly notions about beaux and sweethearts, and if a girl and a boy are seen walking and talking together we either call their attention to the difference of sex by a prohibition, always the effectual means of introducing the very element we wish to hold in abeyance, or we smile and nudge and look conscious, and never rest till our share of the mischief is done, and the boy and girl are prevented from meeting hereafter simply as human beings. Far too

early in life we either consciously and recklessly, or ignorantly and indiscreetly, tangle
up those twisted skeins which are never
straightened out till maturity comes, and the
man seeks the woman and tells her he loves
her, and she returns his love.

During childhood and early youth the love
element should not obtrude itself, nor does
it where the intercourse of boys and girls is
perfectly open, friendly, and taken for
granted ; where it goes on under the eyes of
parents and teachers not by the way of surveillance, but in the normal fashion and
genial atmosphere of the happy home and
healthful school.

One cannot but grant that a marked and
delightful spontaneity of manner, a charm
acknowledged and felt by all who meet
them, is the incomparable dower of well-
bred men and women in the Southern States
of America.   This has been partially explained by the custom of the South, which
from infancy sets girls on a pedestal, with
fathers, brothers, and cousins at their feet to
pay them homage.   But it is further largely
due to the ease and grace of society in the
educated circles of the South and West.
Girls hold their little courts, and boys freely
come and go, with perfect decorum all
around, an absence of deceit, an absence of
familiarity, no sense of indulging in a thing
forbidden, and the pervading but not aggressive presence of parents and older friends im-

parting the touch of distinction which society at its best confers and implies.

The instant one admits the surreptitious, the instant the boy or the girl slips stealthily away from the family, into the dusk, into the garden, into the street, to the highways and the byways, to enjoy the furtive chat, to pay the inane compliment, to venture on the stolen caress which would be ashamed and disgraced should the honest daylight fall upon it,—that instant the serpent has entered Eden and evil has been wrought, evil it may be irremediable, and certainly deplorable.

Our girls and boys are social in their dispositions, and are intended to meet during childhood on a footing of frank and equal comradeship. The tendency of the times, especially in the sharing of wholesome outdoor sports, such as golf or tennis, in which both sexes unite, and in our higher institutions, many of which are either co-ordinate or co-educational, is to more and more emphasize this excellent and safe companionship. When the law came, says St. Paul, "sin revived and I died." Let us be careful not to bring about a condition of things which makes our boys and girls shame-faced hypocrites, by any ill-judged laws of ours which are founded on a misapprehension of God's ordering of society.

Our young people need guidance, need influencing, do not need arbitrary external commandments. In their Christian Endea-

vor Societies and Epworth Leagues, in their
Young People's Unions, wherever they meet
for a common purpose on a common ground,
their intercourse is beyond the reach of the
unkind word, and justifies the wisdom which
at their beautiful age sets them at work together.

People frequently precipitate results which
they never intended by hasty and indis-
criminating interferences, by uncalled-for
comments, and by a general taking on
themselves responsibilities which were not
required.   Sentiment seldom enters into the
social intercourse of boys and girls, unless it
is brought there by the meddlesome hands
of injudicious older friends and spectators of
that game of life which repeats in differing
phases the same story through the swiftly
rolling centuries.

In the home, in the neighborhood, in the
church and in the school, let the boys and
girls meet on equal terms, above suspicion
because without deceit, and they will be
trained, daily and surely and imperceptibly
as flowers and trees grow, for the amenities
of maturer life.   Let us avoid espionage,
which is unworthy, and wholly unnecessary
if parents live with their children and loving
confidence reigns in the household.

## THE DAUGHTER AT HOME.

One of the most beautiful things a girl at home can do is to receive friends graciously. In one's own house a cordial manner is peculiarly fitting and pleasing. One should not stand off in the middle of a room and bow coldly and formally to a friend who has called ; this method has an air of chill and effectually keeps the visitor from being at ease. Walk across the room to meet the friend, extend your hand, and say pleasantly that you are very glad indeed to meet your acquaintance. Stiff, cold, and formal ways of greeting are never proper in a daughter welcoming guests to her father's house.

The daughter of course assists her mother on every social occasion. She pours the tea in her mother's drawing-room when friends drop in at five o'clock, and she assists in every way that she can. She passes the sandwiches and the tea, and takes the cups from the guests who would like to be relieved.

Two distinguished clergymen who were once visiting the poet Whittier were a little surprised and somewhat embarrassed to find Mr. Whittier's niece, a beautiful young

7

lady, the only waitress on the occasion of
the dinner which they had with the poet.
This young lady rose at intervals, changed
the plates upon the table, and did various
little things with a great deal of grace.
"Rather," said one of the gentlemen, "let
us wait upon you." "Not at all," said Mr.
Whittier, "it is our simple American custom
for the daughter of the house to wait upon
the friends of the house, and it is her pleasure
to thus serve you." When dinner was over
the young lady changed her gown and went
off for a ride.

Apart from, and even more important
than, her manner to a guest who happens
in for an hour or a day, is the manner of a
daughter to her parents. The father comes
home at night after a wearying day in business ; he is tired in body and mind. As his
latch-key turns in the home door he throws
off all care, and is joyous at the thought of
the dear ones he will meet after hours of
business.

His young daughter, in a pretty gown,
and with the bloom and freshness only girlhood wears, should be ready to give him
the attentions he loves—the kiss, the cheery
word, and to help her mother and the others
in letting her father see how much he is
thought of at home. Men give up a great
deal for their families—their time, their
strength, the knowledge they have gained
in life's experiences ; they spend everything

freely for their home's sake, and the home
should pay its debt in much outspoken
love.

The daughter at home should practise
small courtesies.

> " Little acts of kindness,
> Little words of love,
> Make our earth an Eden,
> Like the Heaven above."

The daughter of the house when she goes
abroad is the home's representative.  People
judge of her mother and her grandmother,
and the stock she comes from, and the
school she attended, and the companions
she has had all her life, by her behavior in
public.

When you see a group of girls in a cable
car or elevated train who are laughing and
talking so loudly that they attract the attention of every one in their neighborhood, you
feel that they have not been well advised,
for manners in public should be quiet.

If this young woman of whom we are
talking would always be agreeable she will
remember the secret of ease is in not thinking much about herself.  When we entirely
forget ourselves, bashfulness, awkwardness,
clumsiness pass away.  I have heard girls
for instance complain of their height ; they
say " wherever we go, we are taller than the
others."

I do not myself think it a disadvantage to be tall. If one carries oneself well, it certainly is pleasant to be able to look over the heads of a crowd. Tall or short, fat and dumpy, or thin and pale, let no girl or woman think about the impression she is making, either by her diminutive or her stately size.

If possible let the daughter at home have some accomplishment. In these years of musical culture it is no longer enough for a girl to play a little or sing a little, as it once was, but still there is danger that, in our very nicety of knowledge, the old-fashioned music which a girl played for her father and mother and a few friends in the evening is quite dying out. If one can play only marches and waltzes or accompaniments for songs, let her not despise this useful gift ; it adds a great deal to the pleasure of home to have some one there who will sit down and occasionally wake the echoes with something sweet.

The gift of gifts for a girl is expressed in one little word of five letters—charm. I can no more tell you what charm is than I can explain to you what makes the pleasure in the song of the thrush or the delight in the perfume of the rose ; but back across the years I think of this girl and that whom I have known, and I remember one and another who had charm in perfection.

One whose name occurs to me now was not in the least pretty ; she was a little

brown-eyed creature who never dressed
very well, and who slipped in and out of a
room as softly and shyly as a mouse.  The
dear sweet Elizabeth was a perfect fairy in
her home, where she was always ready to
wait upon her father and brothers, where
she was her mother's right hand, where
nothing went on about which she was not
consulted, and where her part was that of
the beloved confidant, who knew all secrets,
and the magician who kept everything as it
ought to be.

In school this sweet Elizabeth was popular beyond all the girls of her class.  She
was constantly in demand, and nothing
could be done without her.  It was, "Where
is Elizabeth?  What does Elizabeth say?
Will Elizabeth be at the party?"  Once
Elizabeth was ill, and a hush seemed to fall
on the town, while people, old and young,
were anxious to know how she was, and
her house was a perfect bower with the
flowers that were daily left for her.

When she went away for a visit, half the
town went to the station to see her off, and
when she returned, the news was told
around household fires, and everybody
came to congratulate her parents on her return.  There were any number of prettier
girls, any number of cleverer girls in the set,
but none to compare with the little, dainty
Elizabeth.

She had charm.  In her case charm was

composed of several elements. Her voice was low, yet clear ; her tones were soft and distinct ; she never had an effect of insisting or forcing herself upon you, yet she was always heard. She was never overlooked, although so gentle. Somehow she always remembered where things had been put, and lost articles drifted into her care. She could explain away small vexations. She remembered people's names and faces—a talent worth cultivating.

Besides, she knew what was going on. She read the best books, listened to conversation about current events when her father and his friends were talking. When she did not understand, she asked a question, and so she had something to talk about and something to tell you when you met her.

I once paid a visit to a farmhouse which stood well back from the road, in a rather lonely situation. The daughter of the house was named Hattie. Her mother had long been an invalid, chained to her couch ; her father was a disappointed man, to whom the world had not been kind. There was a good deal of anxiety about ways and means, and often, I have no doubt, it was quite a problem in that home how to make ends meet ; how to present a good appearance to the public ; how to so turn the old gown that it should look fresh.

But Hattie was equal to any emergency. Her pastor's wife said of her to me : "We

all turn instinctively to that young girl ; she
might be called not only the daughter of the
home, but the daughter of the village, she
has so much common sense, amiability, and
readiness of resource.   In a word, this girl
was possessed of personal magnetism, and
of the delightful quality of all others, which
makes life agreeable, namely charm.

Two very different types of girlhood are
frequently contrasted in our large city shops.
Before the counter, her hands dainty, her
pocket-book filled with money, her dress
like the lilies of the field, stands the girl
who has only to express a wish to have it
granted, who daily eats the best food, sleeps
on a soft bed, and enjoys outdoor exercise
and a change of scene till her bright eyes
and clear color testify to her perfect health
and vigor.

The young woman behind the counter is
often very different in appearance from the
other ; no wonder,—she stands on her feet
for hours at a time, she must be alert, accu-
rate, and accommodating, or she will not
please customers, and if she fails here, she
will lose her position.   Her home is humble, it is often far from comfortable, she
shares her bed with a sister or a child, the
bedroom is the middle one in a tenement,
dark and stuffy, and neither fresh air nor full
sunshine visit it.   When her work is over
for the day she goes out to walk in the nearest park, and there is no pleasant place at

home where she may sit and entertain a caller, or enjoy peace and rest after the day's work.

Of course this is not true of all saleswomen, nor of all working girls. It is true of many. There came to my notice lately the story of one girl, who toiled all day in a store, and in addition paid the rent of a flat in which she and her mother lived, by acting as janitress for the building. Her mother was an invalid, and her salary was so small that it would not cover rent as well as food and medicine. So every morning this girl rose at four o'clock, swept and scrubbed and scoured the stairs and halls, and every evening she hurried home from her work to do what she could for her mother, to light the lamps in her room and the gas in halls, and the day between these duties she passed in service at a notion counter.

A notion counter, you know, is one where you buy pins, needles, buttons, hooks and eyes, tape, elastic, furnishings for a workbasket, corset laces, shoe strings, small wares of all sorts. Don't you think it wonderful that a girl as tired as this one often was, should have gone through the hours of waiting on customers, maintaining amiability and politeness, and always bearing herself with sweetness and gentleness? Sometimes we lose patience with those who serve us. If we could put ourselves in

their places we should learn that they are
handicapped in this and the other way, so
that it is by no means easy for them to be
entirely polite.

Still, some of us have suffered at times
from the indifference, the stony coldness,
and the carelessness of our wishes, shown
by saleswomen, and there are certain estab-
lishments we avoid because of the haughty
deportment of the women employed.
There cannot always be a reason in the
background for the ill-behavior of these
young people ; it must be habit, and lack
of conscience toward their employers and
of responsibility in their spheres of usefulness.  We owe it to them as well as to ourselves, to insist courteously upon our rights ;
and to hold them to the fulfilment of their
obligation.

What we need is the spirit of sisterly
friendship, making each in her place considerate of every other, drawing each to the
other in tender sympathy.  When we pray,
let us pray to lose no opportunity of doing
good, in any humble way that may open
to us ; let us try in Christ's name to do the
best that we can for all Christ's own, where-
ever they may wander.

I found the following bit tucked in a lady's
sewing-basket, cut from her weekly religious
paper, I quote it here, and thus pass it along
as a suggestive word for mothers and girls.

" ' Why don't you let Helen do that sewing?' I said to my wearied friend, who was nodding over a bit of mending. 'Surely she knows how to mend a plain garment like that.'

"'She never has learned to sew,' was the reply. 'She is always busy with her books, and I hate to worry her. She will have a hard enough time by and by. I mean to make her life as easy as I can while she is with me.'

It was so with the dish-washing, the bed-making, the cooking. 'Helen doesn't like to do this, that, or the other. She is out with her friends. She is reading. She is tired. I don't like to make a drudge of her. I don't wish her hands to look like mine.' These were some of the sayings of the mistaken mother as apologies for the fact that Helen never helped in household affairs though there was no servant. Poor Helen! I pitied her from my heart. She was learning algebra and geometry, French and Latin, but was deprived of the sweet lessons in loving help, self-denial, womanliness, and thoughtfulness that only a mother can give in the school of home. Helen was listless, idle, thoughtless, except in school, dependent upon others for the service that every woman should know how to perform.

"What of Helen's future home and the husband whose life she would largely make or mar? What of the possible children whose teacher and trainer she must be? The untrained girl finds endless difficulties before her when she is at last separated from the mother who has waited on her from baby-hood. She has no skill, no deftness, no pleasure in duties for which she is utterly unprepared. The smallest service seems irksome."

## WHEN WE GO VISITING.

Old-fashioned people remember a form of
social visiting which is almost done away
with in our large cities, though it still lin-
gers, I hope, in country places. It used
to be customary for a lady to send in the
morning a little son or daughter with a pleasant verbal invitation which ran in this
wise, the child going perhaps to a half-
dozen friends. Rarely was anything so formal as a note needed for this pleasant and
informal courtesy.

When the door was opened to admit its
round and smiling face, the child would say,
"Mother says will you all kindly come and
take tea with her this afternoon (or to-morrow
afternoon whichever day was preferred), and
meet Cousin Mary, who is paying her a
visit." The less formal asking was for the
same day. The more ceremonious would
indicate the later day.

The ladies would arrive very soon after
an early dinner, at least as early as three
o'clock, four or five o'clock being considered
entirely too late for sociability. They
would bring their fancy work or their knitting, in pretty silk bags. Sometimes one

lady would have on her arm a beautiful and
elaborately beaded bag which was a family
heirloom, and sometimes the work war simply—if too large for ordinary wrapping—
brought in a great roll or bundle, as for
instance, when a woman had on hand a
rug which she was anxious to finish, and
which she even carried to her neighbor's
house. As a rule, however, the work
brought would be trifling and of a kind to
occupy the fingers without needing too much
attention, and eyes and tongue would be
left free for pleasant chat and the friendly
gossip of the neighborhood.

The table would have been set with the
best china before the visitors came, cakes,
golden-brown or rich with fruit, were ready
iced and ornamented, in the pantry. There
would be ham cut in thin slices, delicious
chicken, several kinds of preserves and
pickles, the whitest of bread, and the richest
of cream ; and just before tea time the lady
of the house would slip out from parlor to
kitchen, mix with fairylike swiftness her
favorite style of quick biscuits, pop them
into the oven, and presto ! they would come
out puffs of snowy whiteness, wonderful to
behold and melting in the mouth. And all
would be done like magic, so easily, so
smoothly, and with the minimum of fuss.

About supper time husbands and brothers
would arrive, the ladies would roll up and
put away their work, and a merry company

would gather around the festive board. Usually, the daughters of the house would assist about the waiting on the table, and, if there happened to be no domestic, some of the guests would insist upon helping to clear away the meal after it was finished. But this was not to be thought of and usually the dishes were piled up and left until the evening was at an end, or very likely the best china and the old and prized silver were simply set aside to be taken care of the next morning. The hostess in a dignified manner, gave her whole attention to her guests, as fashion required.

If one lady gave such a tea party as this it would be followed by another, until everyone in the neighborhood had had her turn, and so the pleasant intercourse went on. Many a betrothal was talked over at these parties, many a good thing was set in train, and, notwithstanding a contrary opinion there was very little of either malicious or unkind censure ever expressed in these delightful rural companies.

I think that neighborliness was better understood once than it now is, and yet I am sure that we are still willing to go to the aid of our friends when sickness comes to their homes ; that we care when they have joys ; and that in one way or another people who grow up in the same community learn to know one another's faces and care about one another's interests.

Tarrying a few summers ago in a mountain town of New York, I saw how everybody was interested and delighted in a certain wedding. The young ladies of the place came and decorated the house with flowers, and every detail of the bride's dress and every hour of her happy day was regarded with interest by the entire village from the oldest inhabitant to the youngest child.

But this is a digression. We were wondering whether it is an improvement that the old-fashioned simplicity of our lives has given place in these latter days to something requiring less trouble of preparation, and which in its simplest form is perhaps a good innovation—the ordinary afternoon tea. Some of us think the change a most desirable one. There are teas and teas, however. When a hostess simply asks a few dear friends to drop in at five o'clock and take a cup of tea with her; when she confines her refreshments to thin bread and butter, or small cakes or crackers with the tea; and her daughter or a niece or girl friend, perhaps a maid, helps her to serve her guests, the whole thing being entirely informal, there is no great tax by way of preparation and there is much enjoyment.

Unfortunately, some afternoon teas are, frankly, large and formal receptions, to which crowds of people who do not know each other go; where there is perhaps a

band of music, or, at least, an orchestra
hidden behind portières ; where you cannot
hear yourself speak, because there is such a
chorus of shrill, almost screaming, voices ;
where you simply touch the hand of your
hostess and say a pleasant word and pass
on, and then do not see her again until you
leave, when you have the same brief greeting.   This sort of thing has in it very little
that is satisfying to the soul.

It is the same with visiting.   One used to
go for a leisurely visit to a friend and immediately become a part of the household life.
In the morning the visiting lady would sit
in the kitchen and help her hostess in the
preparation of a meal.   She would perhaps
ask for the mending-basket and give the
tired mother a lift about the little socks and
aprons.   In one or another way, her coming would be a great relief to the house-
mother.

In my own childhood I recollect a dear little lady who used periodically to come and
see us, rarely sending us word beforehand,
but suddenly appearing at our door like an
angel in a brown dress, staying as long as she
wished, and always going away very much
missed and lamented.   There was nothing
she did not take part in, from helping the
children study their lessons to assisting in
whatever entertainments were going on at
the church, or in whatever branch of activity
the friends of the house felt an interest.

As things are managed now, it is not well for anybody to make a surprise visit. Indeed the agreeable person may make it her rule, once for all, that she will not surprise her own mother or her own sister, but will send word definitely if she is planning a visit, telling precisely what train she will take and at what hour she is to be met, and then punctiliously arriving on time.

The lady who wishes to invite a friend, in these days, is careful to mention the length of the visit expected, saying, "My dear Susie, or Jennie : Will you give me the great pleasure of your company from Friday afternoon until Tuesday morning next?" This puts things on a proper footing, so that one knows precisely what is expected of her and can arrange other engagements accordingly.

There are little things which one does well to remember when she pays a visit. One is that at certain periods she would best efface herself and remain away from the family work and the family care, because all households like at times to be alone. She will not criticise the manners of the children nor call attention to any little defect which she may see, as I heard the other day of a very rude guest's doing.

This guest, in the presence of half a dozen people, said to a little boy of the house where she was being entertained, "Freddie

8

dear, if your mother has not time to keep the buttons on your shoes, you come to my room and I will sew them on for you." This was simply an unpardonable piece of interference on the part of a stranger within the gates, who should be blind and deaf to everything that is not quite as it should be. And whose offers of assistance should not imply an unfavorable comment.

The really agreeable person makes it her rule never to make any unkind comments, never to see anything that is not up to the mark, never to hear anything that was not intended for her ; and when she leaves a home where she has had the honor of being entertained, she remembers that by no possibility must she converse with friends about anything unpleasant which may have happened in her presence.

If her friend's house is ill-kept, or her friend's husband is cross, or her friend's children are ill-behaved ; if the dinner was not good or was badly served ; if, in short, anything failed to reach a faultless standard, no sensible or well-bred guest will so much as whisper this in the privacy of her chamber to her other self. Honor requires that we say only kind things of those who have entertained us.

A guest in these days, and in all days, should keep her room in some degree of order while she remains in possession ; it should not look as if a cyclone had struck

it. On the other hand, she is not expected
to take care of the room if there are domestics whose business it is to do this. She
can very easily observe what would be the
best thing in the circumstances and conform her course accordingly.

The best thing we can give our friends
by way of entertainment is not a weary
round of amusement, nor even a constant
progression of picnics and excursions ; to
admit them to the life of the family, to give
them the feeling of being entirely at home,
taken care of and not neglected, is the very
height of modern hospitality.

The entrance of a guest should not greatly
disturb the ordinary routine of a house ; nor
should it be considered necessary when a
visitor comes to stay for a prolonged time
in the home to take her somewhere every day,
to send Jane to sit with her while Ellen is
busy, or in any way to make her feel that she
is an encumbrance or an interference. Usually, the very fact of being under another
roof, of being in a different town and among
different friends, is in itself a solace and a
delight to a visitor.

It is polite always beforehand to tell one's
circle that a friend from another place is
coming, and to specify some hours when it
will be agreeable to have them call upon
her. In these days we often give a reception to a friend, inviting all those to meet
her who would like to touch her hand or

look into her face ; or perhaps to the more intimate ones we give a little dinner or an evening, putting the guest in the place of honor, and in every way showing how proud we are that we have her with us.

The guest should then herself be as entertaining and as gracious as possible. She should be willing to return the calls that are made upon her, and she should not overlook any courtesy shown or trouble taken in her behalf even by the most obscure among the friends of her hostess.

Times change, and modes of hospitality change, but the spirit of true hospitality is the same as it was in the days when Abraham sat at the door of his tent and saw two weary men coming up the road, who proved to be angels unawares.

The presence of an outsider in the house has a certain tonic effect upon every one. We are a little more careful about our manners ; we are a little more careful what we do and say. I remember lately to have read a very suggestive book in which the writer told how he had had a dream in which our Lord Himself came and dwelt in his household as a guest of the home. Instantly there was a different feeling about everything ; the children ceased to bicker and quarrel ; the wife curbed a certain impatience ; the husband restrained a spirit of fault-finding—the whole family lived on a higher plane, and there were many things

which they had hitherto done which they
did not like to do when our Lord was there
to see them. There were many things which
they said of old which seemed no longer
appropriate.

Can we not feel that our Lord is always
our guest; have we no room for Him in our
hearts and in our homes? And this being
so, shall we not day by day tone up our
lives in such a way that we would be glad
and not sorrowful if He should come in
person and knock at our doors? Then,
too, shall we not feel that all our earthly
friendships are hallowed because Christ is
invisibly present at every meal, that the
smallest and most common meal is a feast
and indeed a sacrament because He hallows
it, and that we can have no friendships
worth the having unless they are Christian
friendships sanctified by the one bond which
unites families in heaven and on earth?

## IN CO-OPERATIVE HOUSEKEEPING.

Mrs. Emma J. Gray, writing in *Harper's Bazar*, told the story of family co-operative housekeeping so pleasantly, that, I am sure, no one can fail to be entertained by an experiment which was so successful in its accomplishment.

It is a popular fallacy that relatives cannot comfortably live together—that if the household must comprise more than one family, by all means have the other families strangers; last of all, near of kin. But in the city of New York one member of a large family said to another : " Let us try co-operative housekeeping," which they successfully did.

These relatives were a mother and her bachelor brother, both advanced in years, a young lady daughter and two young men sons; a married daughter and her husband; a younger married daughter, her husband, and her four-year-old son. These people lived co-operatively for several years, in the meantime saving a large sum of money for each family. But, what was of far greater importance, they were able to state, when some of the family were obliged to live out-of-town, and therefore broke up the association, that "throughout the years of our co-operativeness not one unpleasant conversation has occurred. There have been differences of opinion, but no friction; none of the jars that sometimes come between mother-in-law and sons-in-law; between sisters-in-law and brothers-in-law. Indeed, if it were possible, we love each other more than ever."

It was a delight to visit their home—a delight almost equally noted by the stranger-guest and the long-time friend. The warmest hospitality was offered. There was no uncertain welcome. During the years many and varied were the entertainments given; social functions of all sorts were fulfilled, such as evening and day receptions, dinners and luncheons—indeed, the many complex duties as well as pleasures devolving upon the up-to-date, all-around New York woman.

Below is a schedule of their household economy, and any co-operative household may follow it without the least anxiety to the smallest minimum. The only change necessary would be to divide the expenses and work according to the number comprising the particular family.

As in this household the mother was not allowed to be fatigued, she was counted out of all anxiety, worry and work. She, however, paid her part of the expenses. All the rest of what it means to keep house was as-

sumed by her daughters. The letters A B C
will indicate the three families. A's family,
the mother, bachelor brother, young lady
daughter, and two young men sons ; B, a
daughter and her husband ; C, a daughter,
her husband, and little boy. They kept one
maid ; therefore the family in all numbered
eleven people.

The greatest difficulty was the obtaining
of a house with a sufficient number of sleeping-apartments, enough parlor-rooms, and
in a convenient location. But such a one
was found. The house had three parlors,
so that several sets of guests could be entertained at one time without interfering with
one another. It was situated in a good, if
not an aristocratic, neighborhood, very convenient to business, and within five minutes'
walk of the elevated railroad station and
three surface lines of cars ; also, but a short
walk from the Metropolitan Museum in Cen-
tral Park. The rent was eleven hundred
dollars.

PERCENTAGE OF RENT.

A............ .461, per month=$42 26
B............ .256,   "      "   =  23 47
C............ .283,   "      "   =  25 94
                                    ———
        Total amount per month = $91 67

Multiplying $91 67 by twelve, so obtain-
ing the amount for one year, $1100 04 is
found, which, minus the four cents, gives

the exact rent. The rent could not be determined with greater accuracy, and whoever paid the extra four cents one year did not have to do it the next.

The expenses of the house were divided into two classes. Of the first class each bore one-third of the expense.

*Class I.*—Fuel, ice, replacing broken crockery, and buying extra pieces ; house-furnishing, such as brooms, tins, pots, towels, etc. ; servant's wages, extra help, laundry, furnace, street-cleaning, etc.

Of the other class each bore a fractional part, as defined.

*Class II.*—Gas, table supplies, the servant's living expenses and wages, were divided into four parts, of which C took two, one for the little boy, thus paying his expenses. A took one part, and B took one part. When the little boy was away each bore one-third of the servant's expenses, instead of one-fourth as when the child was at home.

The whole amount of table supplies was divided between the number of people at home, including the servant. Each paid as many times the quotient as he or she formed parts of the whole. When one of the family was away, the head of that section, whether A, B, or C, had one less share to pay of the weekly expenses, and so on as the family decreased. When all were on a vacation the head of the family paid one-third of the servant's wages, one-third of the servant's or one person's share, one-third of the fuel consumed. A's share was five people plus the servant, therefore A's share numbered five and one-fourth. B's share was two people plus the servant, which equalled two and one-fourth. C's share numbered herself, her husband, and little son, plus the servant. And as one-fourth was allowed for the child, and one-fourth for the servant, C's share was two and one-half. The gas bill was paid in the same proportion.

But there were many extras. Example : cigars, table waters, anything exclusively used ; special entertainment as dinners and luncheons. These were paid for by the party entertaining or consuming the same.

When guests came for a week or more, such guests practically became members of the household, and A, B, or C added one to the number of the immediate family. General company was not reckoned for at all, because such company belonged as much to A as to B or to C.

Meals were served promptly, the hours being indicated in each sleeping-apartment. A half hour leeway was allowed, but any person coming later found the dining-room locked. The person could gain entrance and have special service, but for the same he was fined ten cents. The total amount received in this way at the end of each year was devoted to charity.

As necessary as is the adjustment of finances is the adjustment of work. Labor, whether physical or mental, should justly fall on each housekeeper. The question of justice is usually a question of conscience. In this household there were the mother, who was not allowed to assume care, and the young lady sister, who seemed far too near the golden glory of life's morning to be tried with the many vexations that come soon enough as life goes on. But, nevertheless, the young sister had an important duty to perform. She was responsible for the marketing through the entire year. When she went on her vacation, whichever one of her sisters had the least at the time to attend to took her place. But the young lady did not herself decide on market necessities ; the sister then the housekeeper gave her a list of what was required. The young lady had no responsibility beyond buying the desired articles. This she conscientiously did, not only buying the best groceries and meats, but obtaining such at the lowest figures. Besides the marketing, she was also responsible for her mother's, uncles', and brothers' sleeping-apartments, and assisted either of her sisters when requested.

The sister known throughout this paper as C was the bookkeeper. The necessity for accuracy in the keeping of such accounts made this task anything but a sinecure. And yet there was much gratification in seeing just how money was spent. All the rest of the housekeeping was divided between B and C, and everything seemed to move upon oiled wheels ; not a discordant sound was heard. If they had annoyances, as they doubtless did, they were wise enough to keep them from being discovered. Indeed, it is doubtful if in the entire city a more thoroughly happy home could have been found.

A youthful matron lately said : "If experienced housekeepers would only honestly tell their methods, what an assistance they would be ! The trouble is there is so much mere talk, and housekeepers don't always care to make full confession. They would rather keep a little back, lest the world should think ill of their various economies."

Altruism surely belongs in the home, though of necessity its limit does not end there. And altruism must always abound in its utmost sense if co-operative housekeeping is to be a success.

It has so often been asserted that no house is large enough to shelter two families, that it is interesting to read about one which made a success of combining the constituent parts of several in one amiable association. I have watched the course of a set of friends of my own, three or four youthful married pairs, who joined their forces, took a large and convenient dwelling, paid their share of all expenses, and found it practicable to

be easy if not rich on a narrow income.
Each matron kept house a month in her
turn, and the result was a large amount of
liberty, an elegant style of living, comfortable
furniture, a nice and well-appointed table
and many luxuries, at a cost less than each
couple would have paid in boarding, and
at the same time with—in the use of a common parlor and separate suites of living
rooms—as much dignity as appertains to
housekeeping.

Only people of congenial tastes and a
standard of expenditure approximately
similar can with any hope of success,
engage in such an enterprise as this. One
disagreeable person might not wreck the
peace of the whole, but he or she would
mar it, and two or three would be fatal.
To bear and forbear in co-operative family
life is imperative, unless it shall prove a
failure.

In order to facilitate the work of a large
family, and to avoid friction in the kitchen,
which has been called the heart of the house,
the different members must conform to
previously decided upon rules. Hours for
meals must be selected and observed.
Punctual attendance at breakfast and dinner ensures the orderly routine of work for
the day ; while little delays, five minutes here,
a quarter of an hour there, put everything
in confusion and wreck the best-laid plans.
The transgreesor in punctuality can never

be agreeable in the true sense of the word, for he is essentially a marplot, causing a break in the sequence of affairs and making trouble all along the line, as if one train should lose time on the schedule, and throw out a dozen others.

Edward Everett Hale, whose true insight is that of a seer, in one of his stories, shows us a lady momentarily hesitating in a Boston street car, and causing twenty people or more the loss of precisely two minutes. She never discovers it, but years after, her fortune gone, her whole environment changed, the poor lady becomes a beneficiary in an Old Ladies' Home, all because she once vacillated in the choice of a shop at which to buy cap ribbons, and her delay blocked the plans of a great many people. For, lo! we are all bound in one bundle and no man liveth and no man dieth to himself alone.

## WHEN FORTUNE FAVORS.

To be light of heart and cheery of mien when fortune favors, seems no great matter ; most people fancy, especially when they are poor and distressed for money, that they could be very good-tempered and quite delightful if only they had a long purse and a good bank account. I am sure we have many friends and acquaintances who think that wealth would bring them great happiness, and that calamity and disaster would flee if only they had a gold mine to fall back upon. Look at the craze for the California gold-fields in '49 ; look at the mad rush to Klondyke now. "When fortune favors," we cry, "then indeed we will look out upon life, and behold everything in *couleur de rose.*"

Yet, quite recently, in his splendid Recessional ode published immediately after the conclusion of Queen Victoria's Diamond Jubilee, the gifted author, Rudyard Kipling, struck a true and deep note. Intended for a lofty national occasion, there is still a word of warning to us in our private and personal capacities, for God's word says to every heart, "In the day of prosperity be

joyful, but in the day of adversity consider.'
We are apt to be selfishly joyful, when
everything is well with us ; and trouble, like
the storm-wind, drives us home to God.

> " Lord God of hosts, be with us yet,
> Lest we forget—lest we forget."

was the burden of Mr. Kipling's solemn
poem. In our time of prosperity, we need
to lay to heart the lesson that riches are
only sent to us in trust, and that we must
one day give an account of our stewardship.

To be agreeable when one has nothing to
be worried over, requires an amount of
strength of mind and of true nobility which
is not the natural endowment of anybody, and this is particularly true when
wealth is not inherited, but is the accumu-
lation of shrewd calculation, and fierce
resolution to win its trophies. Many a
man declares that if he shall ever have a
million, two millions or more, he will be one
of the most liberal givers in the world. But
he does not always carry out his determination. I have often met paupers who wore
purple and fine linen and fared sumptuously
every day ; paupers, for they were poor in
heart and sordid of hand ; they spent only
for their own desires and gave as the churl
gives, grudgingly, to all good causes. "A
single million," said a daintily dressed
woman at an elegant luncheon, " why that
is only genteel poverty."

If we would bear ourselves with irreproachable dignity and real generosity, if we would be truly and in the best sense of the word agreeable, when fortune favors, we must regard money as an opportunity, and its right disbursement as a rare privilege. Our constant feeling must be voiced by the familiar hymn,

> "A charge to keep I have,
>   A God to glorify,
> A never-dying soul to save,
>   And fit it for the sky.
>
> To serve the present age,
>   My calling to fulfil;
> O may it all my powers engage
>   To do my Master's will !
>
> Arm me with jealous care
>   As in thy sight to live;
> And O thy servant, Lord, prepare
>   A strict account to give ! "

Acting on the two strongest lines in that hymn, "To serve the present age," and "A strict account to give," some of the rich Christian men and women of our day, are dispensing their fortunes so wisely and so freely that they send forth rills of blessing in many directions. One woman supports here and yonder, in different cities, free Kindergartens which gather in the small children in our cities, and taking them from the streets, start them in paths of usefulness and honor. Another supports in Europe,

9

gifted and talented young people who are studying music and painting, putting in their hands weapons and tools, by which they may fight or may carve their way to independence. Yet a third has in this and the other college scholarships, which enable worthy and struggling young people to gain a liberal education. A fourth makes of her home a radiant social centre where people come together, talk, enjoy themselves, are rested and refreshed. Such using of wealth proves that one knows how to make the most of a talent committed by God to his hands.

No agreeable man or woman can for an instant be so indelicate as to flourish his wealth or hers in the face of a poorer friend. No agreeable person will, for instance, comment on the inevitable deficiencies in the establishment or the wardrobe of one less fortunate. In every practicable way the agreeable rich person keeps the accident of his means in the background when in society with those whose means are narrower, though socially they are equals. Wealth means, if you please, luxury, opportunity to travel, the choice of many pleasures and diversions, which you may, if you choose, gracefully share with friends, but on which you must not plume yourself. When the question of relative values comes up for final decision, many a poverty-stricken rich man may bewail the blindness with which he fancied that mere gew-gaws had worth beyond the sheen and tinsel of the moment. Bunyan's man with the muck rake, industriously gathering up sticks and straws, and indifferent to a celestial crown, which he never lifted his eyes to observe, is a case in point.

When fortune favors, let us take advantage of the flowing tide to make our homes as attractive as we may both indoors and out. Now is the time to surround ourselves with curios from the East and the West, with rugs from Damascus and Jerusalem, with marbles from Italy, with beautiful paintings, exquisite china and all the books we can afford. One of the most obvious duties for an agreeable man of means is to become a discriminating patron of the arts, buying judiciously, adorning his house, making in it a picture gallery or a library, and in one way or another aiding those who are less well supplied with ducats in the one possible and sensible fashion open to him, by creating a market for their wares. The author and the artist do not, as in good Sam Johnson's and Oliver Goldsmith's day, find a rich patron who becomes an actual sponsor for their works, but rich men are in duty bound to extend patronage to genius by the simple method of buying what genius produces.

Freedom from grinding care, leisure for travel, a respite from incessant toil, ought

to make us very thankful, and very solicitous to be sweet and gracious and bountiful.  Many such sweet and gracious and
bountiful people I know to whom money
is God's recognized gift, and they are dearly
beloved and highly honored in proportion
as they use the gift aright.

Says Bishop Thorold :   " If the first thing
about money is to get it, the second is to keep
it.   And it is not so easy to keep it.   Most
people have some sort of screw loose in their
private money matters.   Either they invest
it foolishly, or they spend it wastefully ; or,
what is almost the worst possible thing to
do with it, they hoard it covetously ; and
either way, it is their Lord's money hidden
down in the earth, instead of being put out
to use for Him.

" The investment of money is just one of
those questions which it is real wisdom to
think over very carefully, till our mind is
made up about it ; and then, when once settled, it should be put away upon a shelf, to
be left there.   Money, like every other talent, is to be made the most of ; and it is our
duty to see that we do make the most of it,
or it is worth just so much less, both for our
own use, and our power of sharing it with
others.

" Few things require more pains, show
more character, or earn more results than the
expenditure of money for household necessities.   Several points strike one here as indis-

putable, but singular. How much more some people spend on mere eating and drinking than others. How this is true, not only of navvies, and pitmen, and artisans, but of persons of all ranks and circumstances. How apt such persons are to complain of their poverty, and that they never have money for anything else. How easily such luxuries come to be looked upon as the indispensable necessaries of life. How the simpler and more frugal people, who would equally like them, but go without them, because other things seem to come first, never get credit for their thriftiness, but are assumed not to mind about them. How little any one gets for his money spent this way, except dyspepsia and a habit of self-indulgence. How quite the worst and silliest way of spending money is to eat and drink it.

'But our household expenditure means other possibilities of extravagance than those of food. Costly changes in furniture, not for being worn out, but for being old-fashioned; what is called 'stylish living,' so often the pretentious vulgarity of pseudo gentle-people, and so miserably and deservedly failing in procuring the consideration it spends so much to buy; an expensive way of entertaining, which gratifies nobody but the tradesmen who supply the goods; servants simply to minister to laziness; and incessant goings to and fro to this place or that, merely because home is dull: these

are items of expense which swell the house
bills of many a quiet family, with little in
return but constant mortification, and the
pressure of debt.

"Lord Bacon, in his Essay on Expense,
clearly points out that 'he that is plentiful
in expense of all kinds will hardly be preserved from decay.' While one hobby, judiciously and moderately indulged, can hardly
hurt a poor man, half a dozen may make
a bankrupt of a rich one. That idiosyn-
crasies of expense have, on the whole, been
beneficial to society, needs no arguing ; since
but for the costly enthusiasm of private,
and sometimes eccentric, collectors, there
would be none of those accumulations of art
and books and sculpture, that give all classes
a share in the enjoyment of their wealthier
neighbors, and sow broadcast the fruitful
seed of many a lofty thought and noble production. This, too, is certain : that pictures,
plate, marqueterie, china, or vertu of any
kind, when really good of its sort, is a valuable investment if you can wait for your interest ; to buy well, even if you pay highly.

"To have just enough, and to know that it
is enough, and to be thankful for it—this is
the secret which the Gospel long ago pro-
claimed to mankind, but which the wisdom
of this world rejects with scorn. Yet to
suppose that a modest competence, such as
modern times would call utter poverty, has
no real charms or vivid enjoyments of its

own, is a profound mistake. It is full of
joy, though of the simplest and purest kind.
Let some of us middle-aged people, who,
after twenty or thirty years' hard work, have
a little more to live upon than when we first
started (though, indeed, we have very much
more to do with it), look back to the days,
long ago, when, in a tiny house, and with
simple furniture, and the whole world in
front of us, domestic love sweetened every
care of life."

## WHEN TIMES ARE HARD.

When times are hard people are apt to lose sight of the fact that material advantages are not the only ones which we ought to care for in this world. Retrenchment is never quite so pleasant as expansion, nor is poverty so delightful as wealth, but the old prayer remains a wise one for us all, "Give me neither poverty nor riches ; feed me with food convenient for me."

Hard times are particularly trying to families which have not felt the pressure of want, and who have been accustomed to an easy and luxurious style of living. To move from a large house to a small one, to learn the fine art of doing without, and to hear quite near one's door the low growl of that wolf who is always anxious to put his head inside if he can, is not conducive to ease of mind and contentment of heart.

Yet to those who have trodden its soil, the valley of humiliation has many lovely spots where the heartsease blooms and fragrant airs blow. The right way to feel about this is not that there is anything lowering in the accident of poverty, and that the day of small things is often the happiest day of one's life.

In hard times, if the family love each other and cling together, the very children share the family spirit, are taken into the confidence of the parents, and rejoice at any opportunity they have to show how fond and dear their affection is and how much they can do to help along.

I was greatly impressed in a visit which I once paid in a section of our country which is less easy and luxurious than it is around the larger cities, with the brave, self-respecting spirit of the young people and with the charming and gracious manner of the older ones. Everyone shared the housework, even the boys willingly taking a hand to help their mother and sisters.

Certainly there is not a more beautiful sight under the blue canopy above us than that of a stalwart youth of seventeen or eighteen who comes jauntily into the kitchen where his sisters are ironing, and, after saying, "That work is too hard for you; let me take a hand," actually begins ironing sheets and towels with the deftness of an accomplished laundryman. This sight is often seen in some New England farm houses of which I know.

My regard for the manly young fellow who did this work in one instance was not lessened by the fact that he was an athlete, riding a wheel, plying an oar, trimming a

sail and sitting a horse to perfection. Nor
have I less respected certain plucky young
women whom I have seen during their summer vacations utilizing the time which was
theirs between terms by accepting service
in summer hotels. "Do the next thynge" is
a good rule for all of us.

Some of the most satisfactory and agreeable weeks I have ever spent in my life
have been in nooks in the Green Mountains
or the White where all the waiters and
waitresses at the tables were college
students. A few summers back when staying at a lovely hamlet by the sea in New
Jersey some of my friends one day found
that all the help in the Inn had suddenly
decided to leave, so that the host was very
much embarrassed, not knowing where to
turn for immediate assistance. But he need
not have been troubled. A bevy of young
men, students at two of the finest colleges
in the country, immediately tendered their
services and for three days held the fort,
performing all the duties which the waiters
had done with an ease and celerity and distinction of manner which was so delightful that the guests were sorry when the
amateur waiters returned to private life and
others of the regular profession came to
take their places.

When hard times come it is just as well to
receive them in a spirit of brave and blithe
heroism. One may always say to one's

self, " After all, what does it matter whether
I have a little more or a little less money, or
what kind of house I live in, so long as my
dear ones are about me, so long as I have
health and strength and pleasure in the things
my eye sees and my ear hears? "

A man many times a millionaire was
looking out of the window of a tall building
one day when he saw on the sidewalk below
a porter carrying heavy bales and bundles
into the shop.  With a pathetic look, he
turned to a friend and said : "All the gold
I have accumulated, all the stocks and
bonds, my whole fortune, I would willingly
exchange for the muscles and sinews, the
strength and vigor, of that man below."
No doubt had the man looked up and known
the condition of the one who was gazing at
him from his vantage ground above, he
would have sighed for the golden wealth.
Yet it would have been a poor exchange
for him.

A few years ago there was a general feeling in the air that in times of family stress
girls were of little use ; that they were simply
ornamental members of the family, to be
cared for and carried on ; and there was a
sort of unspoken feeling that brothers must
be prepared to take care of their sisters at
all hazards.  We often heard, for instance,
of a brother who could not marry because
he had to support several sisters who lived
at home in ease if not in idleness.

This has all been changed, and girls at
an early age, if they do not go to college,
assume, when there is need, some share in
the expenses of the family.   It is very un-
common to find a young woman who keeps
the money she earns exclusively for herself.
Almost always some of it goes into the
family exchequer, and her mother, in most
cases, is the treasurer who dispenses and
dictates what shall be done with the earnings
of the youthful daughter.

Where there are several daughters, they
speedily assume a share of the work and
the cost of the household, and there is no
longer a vision before us of a gray-haired
father bowing painfully beneath the weight
of a number of indolent young women, who
instead are very proud to lend a helping hand.
So, even if there come seasons of financial
depression, there is no need on that account
of our dispensing with the pleasant art of
being agreeable.   Rich people have no
monopoly of that art.   One finds it flourish-
ing and beautiful in homes where money
has little to do with the everyday pleasure.

Of one thing we must be careful, and
that is that when times are hard we suffer
no false pride to make us try to keep up
appearances and live beyond our income.
In no country is there so much wasted as
in ours, and nowhere else do people habitually spend more than they earn as they do
with us.   Half the trouble, half the heartache

which we have to bear comes from the unnecessary strain of trying to make both ends meet when there is no possibility of their meeting. If we simply and frankly recognize the situation, accept the fact that we cannot live precisely as our neighbors do, if we have $1,500 and they have $10,000 a year, we shall then be saved from resorting to many a shameful expedient; and above all we shall not bind our feet with the ball and chain of debt.

To pay as one goes is the best wisdom. It is indeed hard for anyone to be very cheerful when there is always over one's head the menace of some bill which cannot be paid; when, like Dick Swiveller, one dodges around corners to avoid meeting creditors until finally street after street is shut up so that he is forced to creep out of doors in the dark and to hide himself from the face of day.

Far more sensible and much more courageous is the man or woman who decides upon a certain schedule of living and adheres to it. To do women justice, they are often kept in the dark as to the amount they have a right to spend, particularly if their husbands have not salaried occupations or a fixed income, and they are blamed for extravagance when they should simply be pitied for ignorance of the true state of affairs.

Not infrequently the knowledge of a common burden to bear, as when an entire family are endeavoring to pay off the debt which rests upon a home, or when each gladly does without that someone else in the household may be able to carry out a cherished project, draws the family lines closer, and the sense of brotherhood is greater because of the need which has made all one.

It is never quite fair to let one person in the home monopolize all the ease while the others work too hard, yet this one sometimes sees. The selfish person is very apt to take advantage of the kindness shown him or her by others, and there is occasionally found one brother or sister who is perfectly willing to be carried along by the efforts of the rest without making the least endeavor on his own account. I have even known a husband who, belonging to the great army of the unsuccessful, contentedly suffered his wife to bear the burden which should have been put upon his stronger shoulders.

Hard times are only driven away by united effort, united saving, and a common front to the foe. There is no particular use in believing in luck, because when you get to the last analysis there is no such thing as luck. There is such a thing as pluck, and pluck and perseverance together win the hardest battles in this world. May we not take to our hearts the thought which I hope you will find in this little poem?

### THE SILENT MARCH.

When the march begins in the morning
 And the heart and the foot are light,
When the flags are all a-flutter
 And the world is gay and bright,
When the bugles lead the column
 And the drums are proud in the van,
It's shoulder to shoulder, forward, march !
 Ah ' let him lag who can !

For it's easy to march to music
 With your comrades all in line,
And you don't get tired, you feel inspired,
 And life is a draught divine.

When the march drags on at evening
 And the color-bearer's gone,
When the merry strains are silent
 That piped so brave in the dawn,
When you miss the dear old fellows
 Who started out with you,
When it's stubborn and sturdy, forward, march !
 Though the ragged lines are few.

Then it's hard to march in silence,
 And the road has lonesome grown,
And life is a bitter cup to drink ;
 But the soldier must not moan.

And this is the task before us,
 A task we may never shirk,
In the gay time and the sorrowful time
 We must march and do our work.
We must march when the music cheers us,
 March when the strains are dumb,
Plucky and valiant, forward, march !
 And smile, whatever may come.

For whether life's hard or easy,
 The strong man keeps the pace,
For the desolate march and the silent
 The strong soul finds the grace.

A long period of unbroken prosperity is not always the best thing for the soul's growth. "If God saw that we could be trusted with large possessions," said a wise man, "He would certainly give them to us, but He may see that we are only fit to carry on small concerns."

We very often say thoughtlessly that if we had this or that amount which has been denied us, we would be very generous and kind and altogether admirable. Do not let us deceive ourselves. People who are not agreeable in days of ill-fortune and disaster, people who are disagreeable when they have to fight with misfortune and poverty would probably be extremely arrogant and quite unbearable if they had large possessions.

Wealth and poverty, after all, do not touch the real person. The man or the woman, the individual, is independent of such things as these, which will not go out of the world with us, and which will appear in their true light when we come to lay aside this body and to leave the tent in which we have dwelt so long. We shall then find that the things of time have been but as mirage in the desert, and that the abiding things belong to that city which hath foundations and where the streets are paved with gold. "There," as F. B. Meyer has pithily said, "they walk over streets paved with what we here consider the only thing worth having." The ideals of heaven and of earth are probably quite distinct and separate.

## HOPEFULNESS.

Hopefulness, a sanguine turn of mind, a tendency to look on the bright side, are of the greatest value in character. Melancholy, when it becomes a fixed habit, degenerates into insanity, and its evil effects are felt not only by its immediate victim but by every one in his vicinity. The hopeful person is not melancholy, has not the blues, looks cheerily forward, expecting something bright and glad a little farther on, and helping to bring the gladness by the very mental attitude which refuses to see the clouds in the sky.

"Molly Pease is a perfect rubber ball," said a girl the other day, referring to a friend, "You cannot permanently depress her if you try. She is one of those people whose darkest clouds have a silver lining, and it's just a cure for low spirits to live in the same house with her." Blessed Molly Pease.

Of a doctor whom I know a patient remarked "It's half the battle to have Doctor Lightheart come into the room with that jolly face and cheery genial voice of his. He fairly routs the enemy before he writes

10

a prescription ; somehow disease retreats when that sunny look of his challenges it to do its worst."

Now, you perhaps were born hopeful, dear reader, and it may be that you owe much of your happy temperament to some ancestor like Molly Pease or Doctor Light-heart. If this is so, thank God on your knees, for you are equipped for the battle and the struggle, the ups and the downs of life, as only the most enviable and fortunate persons are. Mr. Despondency and Mr. Ready to Halt and poor Miss Much Afraid who came into the world handicapped and hampered by their nerves, their innate bias toward sorrow, their wretched health, or their distrust of the future, are the people to be pitied, not you.

We speak of our dear Lord as a Man of sorrows and acquainted with grief, and we habitually think of Him as walking before-hand in the gloom of Gethsemane and the awful shade of Golgotha. Yet Christ must have been happy. He had the joy that was set before Him, and it glowed like the sun on His path. Evermore He knew that His mission was to be accomplished. The smile of His Father was always with him. So the sick were glad when they heard his voice and the shout " Jesus of Nazareth is passing by" made the blood leap in the veins of the blind, and the children clung to him, and crowded close to him for his bless-

ing. Jesus was a hopeful, a happy, a full-
hearted man, and we please Him, when most
we are cheery and glad.

It's never worth while to worry, you know.
Consider what sort of things we worry
about, and how futile it is to waste strength
and to be disturbed over what may never
happen. You are afraid your ship will never
come in, the ship you sent out freighted
with so much desire, so many ambitions.
Well, maybe not, but the great probability
is that with all sails set and a favoring gale,
that very ship is sailing homeward now.
You are afraid you'll come to the poor-house
at last, and so you save and scrimp and
deny yourself, and never take the good of
your earnings and your hoardings, ever that
ghastly spectre of poverty before you, and
what does it all amount to? A woman I
knew who lived in that state of fear and
worry for thirty years, wearing her old
clothes till they fell into rags and ribbons
and looking like a frump with a toothache
most of the time, and then she died, and her
husband brought home a crowd of giddy
young nieces and cousins to live in the
house, and they all spent like water the
money "Aunty" had so painfully saved.
If she had only hoped a little, what a good
time she might have had.

You are not easy in your mind about
your health. You know your throat is
weak, or your lungs, or kidney disease is in

the family, or there is a tradition that the men or the women of your line die suddenly, or there is something which keeps you uncomfortable, and clutches at your peace with a cold hand in the dead of the midnight. I am sorry for you, but I repeat the Master's words, "Take no thought for the morrow. The morrow shall take thought for the things of itself. Sufficient unto the day is the evil thereof." Do not worry, oh, poor, trembling soul. "Hope thou in God, and thou shalt yet praise him !"

Of all dreadful things, of all heart-breaking experiences, the very worst is living in an atmosphere of hopelessness. Nobody is so trying, so exasperating, so pitilessly wearing as the one who has said good-bye to hope. To dwell with such an one is to live with Giant Despair in his dungeons in Doubting Castle. You have not forgotten what happened to the pilgrims, Christian and Hopeful, when this dreadful giant pounced upon them for their sins of sloth and little faith, and carried them to his dark fastnesses. Bunyan, in his story, so fresh and true to our experience still, shows us how Despair and Diffidence, when they unite their forces, can make havoc with any soul.

"Now there was, not far from the place where they lay, a castle, called Doubting Castle, the owner whereof was Giant Despair, and it was in his grounds they now

were sleeping ; wherefore he, getting up in
the morning early, and walking up and
down in his fields, caught Christian and
Hopeful asleep in his grounds. Then with
a grim and surly voice he bid them awake,
and asked them whence they were, and
what they did in his grounds. They told
him they were pilgrims, and that they had
lost their way. Then said the giant, 'You
have this night trespassed on me by trampling in and lying on my grounds, and therefore you must go along with me.' So they
were forced to go, because he was stronger
than they. They also had but little to say,
for they knew themselves in a fault. The
giant, therefore, drove them before him,
and put them into his castle, into a very
dark dungeon, nasty and stinking to the
spirits of these two men. Here, then, they
lay from Wednesday morning till Saturday
night, without one bit of bread or drop of
drink, or light, or any to ask how they did ;
they were, therefore, here in evil case, and
were far from friends and acquaintance.
Psa. lxxxviii : 18. Now in this place Christian had double sorrow.

"Now Giant Despair had a wife, and her
name was Diffidence : so when he was gone
to bed he told his wife what he had done, to
wit, that he had taken a couple of prisoners,
and cast them into his dungeon for trespass-
ing on his grounds. Then he asked her
also what he had best do further to them.

So she asked him what they were, whence they came, and whither they were bound, and he told her. Then she counselled him, that when he arose in the morning he should beat them without mercy. So when he arose, he getteth him a grievous crab-tree cudgel, and goes down into the dungeon to them, and there first falls to rating of them as if they were dogs, although they gave him never a word of distaste. Then he falls upon them, and beats them fearfully, in such sort that they were not able to help themselves, or to turn them upon the floor. This done, he withdraws and leaves them there to condole their misery, and to mourn under their distress : so all that day they spent their time in nothing but sighs and bitter lamentations. The next night she, talking with her husband further about them, and understanding that they were yet alive, did advise him to counsel them to make away with themselves.

"Well, on Saturday, about midnight, they began to pray, and continued in prayer till almost break of day.

"Now, a little before it was day, good Christian, as one half amazed, brake out into this passionate speech : "What a fool,' quoth he, 'am I, thus to lie in a stinking dungeon, when I may as well walk at liberty ! I have a key in my bosom called Promise, that will, I am persuaded, open any lock in Doubting Castle.' Then said

Hopeful, ' That is good news ; good brother,
pluck it out of thy bosom and try."

''Then Christian pulled it out of his bosom,
and began to try at the dungeon-door, whose
bolt, as he turned the key, gave back, and
the door flew open with ease, and Christian
and Hopeful both came out.   Then he went
to the outward door that leads into the castle-
yard, and with his key opened that door
also.   After that he went to the iron gate,
for that must be opened too ; but that lock
went desperately hard, yet the key did open
it.   They then thrust open the gate to make
their escape with speed ; but that gate, as it
opened, made such a creaking that it waked
Giant Despair, who hastily rising to pursue
his prisoners, felt his limbs to fail, for his
fits took him again, so that he could by no
means go after them.   Then they went on,
and came to the King's highway, and so
were safe, because they were out of his
jurisdiction."

There is always the way out by prayer,
and promise for the hopeful soul.

''Look up and not down.
Look out and not in.
Look forward and not back,
And — lend a hand!''

## INTERESTING PEOPLE.

The quality which makes a person interesting is not very easily defined or analyzed.
That wonderfully subtle thing which we
call charm eludes the dictionary, is not the
same in one person as in another, and is
not in the least dependent upon either beauty
or youth. The interesting woman, for
instance, may be a trifle more pleasing if
she have a graceful carriage, and a lovely
face ; but on the other hand, we have all
seen scores of women with faultless com-
plexions and very much to pride themselves
on in the way of style and good looks, who
yet failed to interest any one in the world
except their kinspeople and neighborly
friends, for any length of time. Old friends
and neighbors are apt to be loyal and to
excuse faults.

One of the most successful hostesses
and brilliant talkers whom this generation
has seen, was, in fact, a woman of
remarkable plainness, with an insignificant presence, a muddy complexion, car-
roty hair, and nothing to boast of in the
way of stature. Of her, an acute observer
said : "She is simply the most fascinating

person in any company, and wherever she goes, a crowd of delightful and delighted people may be seen gathered about her.

What this lady would have been had she been endowed with personal beauty, I do not know. As it was, she triumphed over many defects, and, to the last day of her life, held a court whenever she chose to grace a drawing-room.

The most faultlessly handsome woman whom I remember, bearing herself with a distinction worthy of a duchess and dressing always in the latest fashion, was so insipid and flavorless and had so few ideas that after having given her the attention one bestows upon a fashion plate, one turned away to forget all about her presence in the room. She was tedious to a degree. The woman who is truly interesting—or for that matter, the man—will constantly add something to the charms already possessed. The Bible rule, "To him that hath shall be given," cannot but be fulfilled in the case of these happily constituted folk. It is well worth while to consider what are the constituent parts of their heaven-born gift and to inquire whether or not it is within our grasp or beyond it.

In the first place, the interesting person did not crystallize at a given point in her career. Sometimes, people cease to make fresh additions to their mental stores and therefore cease to assimilate knowledge and

their minds become in a sense atrophied at
an early period of their lives.  Which of us
has not encountered gray-haired women
who were simply the fossilized remains of
girls of eighteen.   They had not given their
minds anything to do ; they had not remained
receptive to the ideas and the influences
around them ; and in a world full of novelty,
full of stimulus, full of the miraculous in the
way of discovery, progress and invention,
they had ceased to grow.  Such people could
not by any possibility remain interesting.
They were pre-ordained to dulness.

Hard work and incessant struggle have
the effect at times of paralyzing the bright-
ness of a disposition and of changing a
temperament so that one finds, and one
breaks one's heart to find, the mother who
has been outgrown by her children, or the
wife who is no longer her husband's fit companion.  This could hardly have happened
had she, amid all her cares, kept herself in
touch with the younger lives and not allowed
John to separate his life from hers.  For a
good example of the woman who kept her
queenly hand on the helm, I must refer you
to that dear book lately published, " Margaret
Ogilvie," in which the gifted Scotch novelist,
J. M. Barrie, relates the beautiful history
of his mother's life as it was lived in the little
Highland home with her children.  Hers
were everyday the spontaneity, the sparkle,
the vivid interest which made the home

always blithe, and the result was a character interesting to the latest day of its existence upon earth, though at last she was fragile and old. If we would be *interesting*, we must be alive, we must care about things, we must not be entirely absorbed by the routine of petty affairs. I would earnest'y say to the beloved young girl : Cultivate those qualities which will make you invaluable at home and in society, and begin doing so before you leave the school-room. To the elderly woman in danger of too much devotion to her little children and of too greatly narrowing her life within domestic limits, I would again say : Begin to interest yourself in those things which go on outside of your own door. Take time to read and to study even if it be only in snatches, a few minutes now and a few minutes later. Talk with your husband about something more than material affairs, and occasionally surrender the baby to some other hands while you go for a walk or a visit or enjoy some diversion which pleased you before your marriage. Escape into the larger life. The same advice, changed or modified by circumstances, may apply to us all. No one ever grows too old to take an interest in life, and life presents just the largest interest in the fullest measure to those who seek for its best opportunities and gifts.

It is quite worth while to keep up by a little regular practice, the accomplishments one has gained in youth, and a fad or a hobby is not a bad thing so long as it is used by way of relief and not as the one thing in life.

The truly interesting person is not exclusively occupied, however, with herself and her own affairs. As Mrs. Browning says in her sweet poem, "My Kate," "It was her thinking of others made you think of her." No one can be interesting whose horizon is bounded by the insistent *ego*. We must live outside of ourselves, and the more we can do this, the more we shall draw others to us. The secret of being thought what one may call winsome, is in living lovingly and unselfishly in this world, remembering from day to day, that we pass this way but once.

The ability to tell a story delightfully is invaluable to one who would be popular in society or pleasing in conversation at home. People either can or cannot tell stories well. If having tried and failed a number of times, you discover that this is not your talent, you would better leave story-telling to those more highly dowered in this direction. Nothing is more forlorn than to hear a story from which the unfortunate *raconteur* has omitted the point, or a story which is introduced at the wrong moment, or tacked on to the conversation with the evident intention of telling a story because you know it, whether it fits into the woof of the evening or not.

Still, in this desert land there are bright
oases where the story-teller pitches her tent,
and where she enthralls all listeners by the
magic of her words.  Always, there are men
and women gifted as was she who for a
thousand and one nights entertained the
despot against his will, so that he was obliged to forego his savage intent and spare her
menaced life.  A pretty story is told of an
elderly English gentlewoman who was the
guest of the blind King of Hanover.  She
was once driving with the king and queen
when suddenly the horses started and the
carriage seemed about to upset in the middle
of a most entertaining narration.  "Why
do you not go on with your story?" inquired
the king.  "Because, your Majesty, the carriage is just going to upset."  "That is the
coachman's affair," replied the king.  "Do
you go on with your story."

A very charming thing was said about the
wife of Dean Stanley, whose universal cordiality of manner and delightful charm of
conversation are remembered by a very
large circle, constant reference being made
to them in those memoirs of distinguished
people which have repeatedly come from
the hand of Augustus Hare.  Of Lady
Augusta Stanley it is said that her goodness,
wisdom, and tact were always in evidence
and won all hearts.  Going soon after his
marriage to visit a friend, Dean Stanley rode
on the box of the fly.  "I see you've got

Lady Augusta Bruce inside," said the friend;
"I remember her very well at Windsor."
"Not Lady Augusta Bruce. She is Lady
Augusta Stanley now. She is my wife."
"Well, then, I do wish you joy, for your wife
is just the best woman in England !" This
was praise which the dean appreciated.
Somebody may read this and say to herself:
"Years ago I might have developed a side
of my character which would have made
me as delightful as these people of whom
one reads, but it is now too late." Believe
no such thing, dear friend. It is never too
late to improve what is imperfect or to repair
a mistake. To a lady who came with a
story of danger and difficulty to a philanthropic woman this word was said, in
another connection it is true, but it is just as
well worth while in this connection as in
any other :   "My dear, if you stand counting
the difficulties whenever there is a good work
before you, you will never do anything that
is worth doing all your life. Only begin,
begin, begin, and the difficulties will all
disappear."

If we never were taught in early childhood
to yield the best chair and to bring the foot-
stool, to pay small and graceful attentions, to
avoid interrupting another person, to behave
with tact and sweet friendliness, we must
not calmly elect to be clumsy and rough the
rest of our days. The lessons of courtesy,
tact, and good-breeding are easily learned,

and politeness soon becomes a second nature, if it did not happen to be our nature at
first. Anybody may be charming who cares
to be so. It is a matter of prayer and pains.

## AGREEABLE IN ILLNESS.

Most people fancy that the ordinary conventionalities and rules of politeness may be
suspended when they are ill.  A person
who is ordinarily amiable and gentle in
speech and manner allows herself, or still
oftener himself, to be cross and unreasonable
when on a bed of pain.  Of course it is not
easy to bear aching nerves, the unrest of
fever and the general demoralization which
comes when the body is tortured and the
mind enfeebled by disease.  Not even a saint
can be said to enjoy sickness.  The fact is
that in a world adjusted to right conditions
there would be nothing but health and pleasure which comes from a thoroughly perfect
adaptation to the work of the day.  If we were
all well-born and well-reared, if we could
have chosen our own grandfathers and
grandmothers and regulated the way our
ancestors lived, if even from our own childhood we had eaten and slept and labored
and rested with a view to health and right
living, we should probably be able to throw
physic to the dogs and do away with the necessity of the doctor and the nurse.  As it
is, however, there will probably continue to

be more or less illness in this world, more or less pain and suffering ; and however tenderly we may regard our friends and kindred when they are ill, in our own persons we must feel that we have an obligation to behave patiently and with amiability even if we do not feel very comfortable.

Of course it is not to be expected that a man or woman in extreme suffering will have very many little bits of courteous conversation or small change of repartee and anecdote ready for those who are about him or her. The minimum of speech is appropriate at such a time and one may be pardoned if one does not always say, "Please" and "Thank you" : but one is not excusable for irritation, gruffness, and a general bearish rudeness and sharper waspishness of demeanor in illness. All rules are not suspended even then. The mind has a great deal to do with the body at all times, and if one can maintain a placid and tranquil mental state or can repress the outward manifestation of fretfulness, very much will be gained.

Parents owe it to children to begin when the little things are small to teach them that sickness is not a time for crossness. We are all creatures of habit ; habit and training make the difference between the gentleman and the boor ; and habit is made up of the ten thousand little acts, small expressions and trivial affairs which eventually become automatic and result in sweet-

11

ness of demeanor or in the awkward and
clumsy appearance of the untrained and ill-
taught person.

I have known instances in which the long
life of an invalid was so sunny, so beautiful
and so heroic that her presence was a benediction in her home and a joy to all about
her. One such was the case of my own
dear and saintly mother, who for twenty-
five years of her life was seldom free from
pain and who, for winter after winter, was
shut into her home away from the activi-
ties she loved. Always her room was a
place so inviting and so hallowed that her
friends sought it as they would have sought
a shrine. The little child, the bright young
girl, the student just at home from college,
the man worried with business cares, her
pastor, her friends in the church, her children and grandchildren, always came to her
for sympathy, counsel and companionship,
and never came in vain. Once I remember
to have gone to her in the evening just before the hour to say good-night, and I shall
never forget the beauty of her lovely face
and the uplifted look in her eyes as she
said :

"Let me tell you what a beautiful vision
I have had. I lay here between sleeping
and waking—it did not seem to me that I
was asleep, though perhaps I was—but all
at once there was a presence in my room,
something beautiful and splendid. And as

I looked, the darkness grew brighter and brighter as if a rose were unfolding, and I felt as if about me were brooding white wings of angels ; and then I heard a sweet voice say clearly in my ear : ' Be not faithless, but believing.' "

Dream or vision whichever it was, to that angelic melody and sweetness my precious mother's life was set.   And so it continued to be until one winter day, she passed away and went to her home in that land where the inhabitant shall nevermore say : " I am sick," and where her eye forevermore beholds the King in his beauty.   To us who remember her, and to those of her own blood it seems a duty unforgettable to be patient and lovely and considerate and agreeable even in illness and pain.   She was all this, and so must we be, following her bright example.

Years ago, there used to pass my door a bright girl on her way to school.   She would look up as she tripped by the window and toss me a kiss from her finger tips and smile.   She would run in on her way home and sit down for a few minutes and tell me a story of herself.   A brilliant, beautiful, bewitching creature she was, full of plans, hopes and ambitions.   She meant to have a great career, and perhaps she would have done so, but that the year after her graduation, a man, in every way worthy, fell in love with her and gained her maiden heart.

I was a guest at her wedding, and never was bride lovelier, never did a new home build itself on fairer prospects for the future. By and by, there came to it God's precious gift of a little child; and then the life in the little household was sweeter and fuller than ever. As the mother cradled her babe it seemed as if the Madonna look in her face grew and grew, and it was worth going far to see the pretty picture made by the lovely young mother and the beautiful child. She was sitting in church one day, when suddenly she felt a sharp and mysterious pain in her foot. The pain speedily became unbearable. She was taken home and medical skill was sent for, but the strange twinge she felt was the first danger-signal of a mysterious spinal disease which before long laid her upon her couch and which ever since has baffled all the skill of all the doctors who have tried to do anything for her. From youth to middle age this woman has been a prisoner upon her bed, unable to turn herself, unable to hold a book in her hand, unable at some times to bear so much as the pressure of the sheet upon her body without great suffering. Her boy has grown from childhood to manhood accustomed always to see his mother smile at him her good-mornings and good-nights from the bed on which she lies. Her husband, always devoted and almost angelic in constant and unremitting care, has over and

over again said: "I have had a saint for
a wife during all these years, and have known
the joy of heaven in my home except for
the pain which she was bearing and which
I could not relieve." From her couch, this
lady has directed the affairs of her home,
managing its every detail with precision
and fidelity. She has kept herself aware of
what was going on in the world through
books, having them read to her; she knows
the new authors as well as the old. She
has talked with the teachers and professors
who have educated her boy and herself has
influenced every step of his progress; and
to-day, sweet, pure, uncomplaining and un-
failingly cheerful, she meets the visitor with
the brave look which shows how the soul
may dominate the body. If she has learned
the art of being agreeable under all circumstances, what may not you and I do who
have lesser burdens to bear?

Perhaps no malady is so terribly relentless in its demands upon our patience as one
which compels the sufferer to live always
under the menace of the knife. I have
known a woman to undergo repeated surgi-
cal operations, dwelling for years in that
valley of the shadow from which the only
escape is through surgery or death, and
during the entire time have seen her not
only the pattern of courage and fortitude,
but the blithe companion of her children and
often the most entertaining member of her

family. Such a friend I remember to have, for
nearly ten years, kept her entire household
cheerful and bright while she herself was
seldom free from suffering, and when over
and over again she was carried to the hospi-
tal and placed under an anæsthetic, not knowing whether she would ever waken again on
this side the grave.  Such examples rebuke
us for showing impatience in the sudden and
transitory attacks which come to us, or in the
occasional break in life which is made by a
spell of illness.  Fortitude is heroism. Heroism is a matter of faith, of courage, and of
the indomitable will.

There is a way of looking at life which enables one always to be bright and lovely and
charming.  " I have learned the secret," said
St. Paul, " in whatsoever state I am, therewith
to be content."  It is not easy to be content
when you lie in your bed and are aware that
Bridget is wasting the coal, scorching the
linen and breaking the dishes downstairs ;
nor if you have to forego a pleasant engagement, or must lay aside important work because an inconvenient disease of some sort
has fastened itself upon you.  Can you always acquiesce without an inward murmur ?
My point is, that though we feel this murmuring desire, it is in our power to repress
the outward expression of fretfulness ; we
must never forget that in this world nothing
is so contagious as example.  A little girl
was looking out of the window when a rude

boy, passing by, thrust out his tongue and made a face at her. Instantly, she began to cry and her sunshine was gone. But her mother said, "Look out of the window again, my dear, for there comes a pretty young lady." The young lady looked up at the little one, laughed and threw her a flower, and instantly the child was good-humored and happy again. One never knows how far the influence of one's life may go. No story is ever finished in this world. We are all of us living in a story without an end, and as we go along we are, here and there and everywhere, affecting people's lives, doing people good or doing people harm, because, whether we think it or not, we are all bound up in one bundle and each life is in touch with all.

We that are strong should bear the infirmities of the weak, and therefore nothing is more shocking and unpardonable than for those who are well to lose patience in their turn with those who are ill. The caretaker must keep herself serene and self-poised, and, no matter how trying her patient may be, it is her part to be always tranquil and calm. She cannot do this if she is always tired out, or if she foolishly neglect to get what rest she can. When illness enters a family and it is not practicable to have a trained nurse—always the best thing to do if it can be managed—the members of the family should divide the care among themselves and so order things that no one person shall bear too heavy a load. By a judicious arrangement of times and seasons, of night nursing and day nursing, one may relieve another. It is especially needful in time of long illnesses when the campaign, so to speak, extends over months, that outside of the sick-room, there shall be the regular going on of the days and the meals in their proper order, and an opportunity should be made for the nurse, whoever she may be, to get rest and exercise in the sunlight at some stated period every day.

When the caretaker is fussy or imperious or in any way ruffled, her mood reacts unfavorably upon her patient. We may show irritation sometimes in the quality of the voice when the words we use are what they should be. Tones reveal moods, and voices are characteristic. The thing to do is not to *feel* the irritation, and this can only be effected by a sensible and constant taking care of one's-self.

If all our lives were set to the note in which there is neither fret nor jar but only peace and goodwill, what a divine place the earth would be! Every one of us has the right to have heaven in her heart, in her face, and in her home. "The Kingdom of Heaven is within you," and it does not matter very much whether the environment be elegant or simple, the home stately or lowly, if the heavenly spirit be there.

Our Lord is willing to make us his earthly
habitations, and he is incarnated again and
again in his followers. We never read that in
his beautiful earth-life he suffered the pangs
of illness. He seems to have had a perfectly
strong body, able to bear fatigue and trouble and trial to the end ; but we know that
he had great sympathy with and compas-
sion for the sick because he went up and
down the hills and vales of the Holy Land
always healing the sick, restoring sight to
the blind, making the deaf to hear, and,
strangest work of all, casting out devils from
those who were possessed of them. There
are devils still to be cast out, though we
call them by politer names. Fractiousness,
jealousy, envy, perversity, what are these
but demons which sap the heart-life and
make the home-life such a worry? Our
blessed Lord has power still to cast these
out and he still says to every one of us :
"Ask, and it shall be given you."

## AGREEABLE IN OLD AGE.

Some years ago at a country house not
many miles from London, a brilliant man
of letters, one of the class whom Robert
Burns described as "the chiel amang us
takin' notes," was one of a large company
of guests.  It was whispered about that an
old lady was coming, an old lady who
would have travelled straight through from
Scotland and who would probably arrive
perfectly exhausted.  The dinner hour came,
and with it, there glided in amongst the
company, "a graceful, refined old lady with
features the color of white alabaster, in a
black velvet dress, a chain and cross around
her waist and a lace headdress which was
neither vail nor hood, but was so infinitely
becoming to the wearer that from the first
moment of seeing her in it, it was impossible to imagine her in anything else.  She
was soon in conversation, the animation
and inspiration of her eye speaking even
more powerfully than her lips ; and the
next day, the whole party were at her feet.
Her conversation grew hourly more en-
chanting."   This lady was Mrs. Duncan
Stewart, at that time past her seventy-fifth

·ear. In many aspects of her life, she was the typical and ideal old lady, a queen to her latest day. Her biographer says that no one could be with her without feeling better and without showing the best side of his or her nature. She had the habit of looking at the best side of people and she always shut her eyes to their faults. The simplest present or kindness shown her by any one was appreciated. Even if the gift were worth nothing and cost little, she would speak very warmly of the kindness. However much a thing pleased her, she would always rather give it away than keep it for herself. To extreme old age, she retained a happy quality of eagerness about things and some one asking: "Is life worth living?" she replied: "Yes, to the very dregs!" It might have been said of her when at last she passed peacefully and painlessly into the other life :

"From the banquet of life rose a satisfied guest,
   Thanked the Lord of the Feast and in peace went
      to rest."

Old people have the best right in the world to be agreeable, because, in the first place, they have borne the burden and heat of the day and have reached that period when it is right that they should have repose ; because they have experience ; because they stand in the forefront of the generation and are nearer Heaven than the rest

of us. It must be owned that they are
sometimes difficult to please and that there
are not a few of them who invite the opinion of the small boy who said he didn't
want to go to Heaven if grandpa was to be
there. More than young people, the aged
need to guard against any carelessness
about their personal appearance. They
should, so far as they can, keep themselves
up ; their clothing and personal appearance
should always be neat ; and they should be
a little patient with younger people who
seem to them to be forcing attentions which
they do not wish to receive. It is almost
an unfailing sign that one is growing old
when one begins to be sensitive with regard
to help that is offered and to find trifles bur-
densome which were once little thought of.
—"The grasshopper has become a burden."
Even then, one may curb one's irritability
of temper, speak gently and kindly, and
accept the pleasures of the present without
repining over that which has forever gone
by.

In my mental gallery I have several por-
traits. One is of a gentleman of the old
school, ninety years old, when I called at
his house one day, and I still recollect his
full form, his benignant countenance, and
his rising when I came to his chair. To
one who brought him a gift of grapes, clus-
tering purple and sweet on their stems, he
said, "My dear, this was a beautiful thing

for you to do, to bring this fruit to me, you
so young, to me, so old." He cared enough
about a young man to ask if he had been
promoted in his business, and he inquired
whether the little son of a certain poor
woman, had been taken on as an errand boy
in a shop where there had been a vacancy.
Another, an old lady, "Aunty" a town full of
younger people affectionately called her,
held to extreme old age the admiration and
regard of a host of friends. She was never
"blue" or depressed. Her taste for gay
dress amused the younger generation, for
her caps, when she was well past eighty,
were trimmed with bows of pink, and blue,
and yellow, and lavender. "I like the
sweet peas," she said, "they are so light
and airy. Flowers are not sad-colored, and
why should I be so, since I am the happiest
woman in the whole state? I have had a
long life, and a fine one, and I'm going on
to a better country."

Dearest and sweetest of all women of
whom I have ever heard was one who held
the reverent love of the children in a town
well hidden from the great world in a nook
of the Green Mountains. This lady was
called grandmother by everybody. The
girls told her of their love affairs, the young
men consulted her about the choice of a wife.
If somebody's bonnet was unbecoming she
brought it to grandmother who speedily saw
what was amiss and remedied the matter.

A church sociable, a wedding, an evening party or a sleigh ride had the details arranged in grandmother's room, and when she died all the stores were closed, and the schools were suspended on the day of her funeral, while the whole town was in mourning, and the children in long procession carried flowers to line and heap upon her grave,— the grave of a winsome and saintly grandmother. Such a one we have all known and we sympathize with a woman who writes:

"I look back through the mist of years and see the dear old-fashioned farmhouse, lichen-covered, and the morning-glory vines still climbing up the front window, hanging their bell-like blossoms out to the kisses of the sun.

"I can see myself again a child, plucking off the flowers a day old, and 'popping' them. Who has not 'popped' morning-glory blossoms? And then the crab-apple trees that in May sprinkled the door-yard grass with snow, sprinkled the passing breezes with fragrance rare, and oh! so wondrously sweet. Behind the house with its lath fence running all about, to keep out the investigating hens, which mother always declared were the pests of her life, was the garden, with great beds of Johnnie Jump-ups and early crocuses, with sweet peas climbing up the fence and a great sweet brier drooping over. Every corner held some sweet surprise for the summer sun to reveal; here a bunch of Bouncing Betts, or maybe Black-eyed Susans peeping up; a spike of larkspur, or a waving spray of bachelor's buttons.

"I can see them all, the daffodil, the snap-dragon, the marigolds, the dahlias, and the sweet old-fashioned pinks. The lilac tree by the path where birds were ever nesting. And more than all this the rows of currants, blackberries, and grapes; the raspberries and gooseberries; the little corner devoted to strawberries, that mother guarded as the apple of her eye, and then all those dreadful herbs, and the caraway bush and coriander that filled the pockets of our little pinafores with seeds, spicy and delicious.

"After all there was no place on earth so dear. There never can be another. Time brings many changes. The old home has fallen into decay; the last spray of the morning-glory vine has rotted from the front window. The fence that guarded the little garden has fallen away, and rank weeds take the place of pinks and daffodils; and the birds, I even doubt their nesting longer in the lilac by the path. There are no thoughtful hands to hang bundles of herbs to dry above the kitchen stove. All, all, is changed. Oh! time in your ravaging flight what will you leave to us out of all that is dear?"

Last winter in Brooklyn, where I live, there was an Authors' Reading given for a charity.

There was a very long programme and the audience began to show signs of weariness before it was ended. At the very last, when it was late, and the people unmistakably tired, a beautiful old lady,—a lady frankly owning to seventy years,—with her soft white hair and her plain black gown and her face as serene as a summer's morning, came forward and read us a story. She beguiled us from our weariness ; we forgot the hour, we were children at her feet, and the engaging sweetness of this stately and queenly grandmother was the crown of the whole entertainment. This fair woman had never abdicated her throne. Her sceptre abides in her hands. She will be charming to her latest day.

The pretty incident which follows, I clipped from a paper for my scrap-book, and I fancy you will like to read it too.

"The car was crossing the city from the west to the east when a very young mother, evidently from the poorer class, got into the car. Both she and her baby wore the positive evidences of refinement. The modesty of the bonnets worn by each, the daintiness with which the plain clothes were worn, all showed the woman to be one in spirit above her class. The little girl was just beginning to talk. She looked long and earnestly at an old woman, dirty, scowling, and repulsive, on the other side of the car. The child looked so earnestly at the old woman that

the mother thought, perhaps, that was the
reason why the old woman was scowling,
and she tried to attract the little girl's attention, but it was useless. The big blue eyes
were not removed from the face of the old
woman. At last the little girl became so
restless that the mother stood her on her feet
by her knee, when the child, with a quick step
and outstretched arms, threw herself against
the scowling old woman and said, in her
sweet baby tones, ' I dot dranma home ;
me loves dranmas.' The old woman was
so startled at this unexpected display of affection and interest that her eyes filled with
tears, and, putting one hand on the child's
shoulder, she pushed her gently from her
knee, and said, ' I'm not fit fer yez to touch,
child, ye're so sweet and pretty.' But the
baby, with that clear look of innocence that
is so startling in some children, pushed
away the detaining hand and again leaned
heavily against the old woman. This time,
putting her elbow on the old woman's knee
and her chin on her hand, she gazed with
the most bewitching smile into the old
woman's face, murmuring again, ' I loves
dranmas.' The tears overflowed and trick-
led down the cheeks of the old woman, and
there was not a dry eye in the car. The
little mother, with rare wisdom, let the angel
of mercy alone, and there the child stood,
finally taking the corner of the old woman's
shawl in her hand, smiling her friendliness

12

into the face of the woman who evidently years before had built a wall between herself and the world's good-fellowship."

Here, too, is a bit of wisdom from the book of experience. "Because Thou hast been my help, therefore in the shadow of thy wings will I rejoice," cries many an aged saint of God.

"I think we had better keep a book of remembrance, daughter," said my father, as we sat beside our evening fire, rehearsing some unusual perplexities and sorrows. Life had gone very hard with us that year, and I had become a chronic complainer. Just now brother John lay helpless with a broken thigh, and she, who could "run smooth music from the roughest stone" with ceaseless love, had been taken from our sight.

"A book of remembrance, father? Why, I thought the Lord kept that."

"Yes, but why shall not wayworn mortals keep one also, in which to note His gifts ; to recount the blessings of the way ; the 'red-letter' days of sunshine after storm and darkness, joy after sorrow, quiet and peace after confusion, unexpected good, deliverance from danger? It has become easier to speak of our misfortunes and trials than of our blessings. These are received in silence. I'm afraid we shall never become 'housetop saints' at this rate."

"Don't say 'we,' blessed old father!" I

cried penitently, noting with a pang the
glory of swift-coming translation all over
the noble head and face. Smiling at my
eagerness, he softly repeated,—

" Every lifetime,
Yes, the narrowest and most drear,
Is a cup that still runs over
With the gifts of God most dear ! "

"Suppose we take these pocket diaries
and write in them 'Gifts versus Losses,'
blessings over against trials, joys more than
griefs. and see what comes of it.   I think it
would prove no small aid to our happiness
and spiritual health."

A very tender and penitent heart made its
first entry that night in the little book.   On
the fly leaf my father's familiar hand had
written,

" Here, then, inscribe them, each red-letter day !
Forget not all the sunshine of the way
By which the Lord hath led thee ; answered prayers,
And joys unasked ; strange blessings, lifted cares ;
Grand promise echoes !  Thus each page shall be
A record of God's love and faithfulness to thee ! "

It was strange after that, how my book
of remembrance filled up.   I soon had to
have another.   Sometimes I compared mine
with father's, who said,

"You see, daughter, we do not need to
search for His gifts ; they are legion to those
who have open hearts."

Often we found we had mentioned the

same gift or deliverance, but oftener the
need of individuality or experience had recognized what the other had missed.   Where
I had noted gifts of bread and loving-kindness, my father had offered thanks for the
gift of chastening and hidden manna.   Underneath the former he had written : " Courage ! ye who bear the sublime lot of sorrow.
God wills it.    It is the ordinance of infinite
love, to procure for us an infinite glory and
beatitude ! " and beneath the latter : " We
have meat to eat, that ye know not of ! "   I
noticed a spirituality in his remembrances
that marked him, indeed, " a house-top
saint."   Not a day passed, but I had occasion to take my little book many times from
my pocket, note a sweet surprise, a gracious
gift, unexpected strength, or cheer, or light ;
a soft air, a radiant sunset, a perfect day,
an hour of peace, an answered prayer ; an
hour of fellowship, a friend.

## THE GIVERS OF ADVICE.

Advice is cheap, but as a rule it is wisest not to give it unasked ; even when it is solicited, the part of wisdom is to hesitate before bestowing it, as, usually, people invite counsel, wishing to have their own judgment confirmed and determining on the whole, to take their own way. Nobody is so much dreaded as the person who forces advice on his friends, and who persists in dictating a course of proceeding to those who do not in the least wish to hear any voice except their own.

The giver of advice need not expect to be included in the list of agreeable people, for he does not belong there. He is much more likely to be found in company with the unfortunate person who answers in the affirmative, with innocent candor, the friend who says guilelessly, "Tell me my faults ! " Few and far between are those people who can bear hearing their faults told them even by the lips of friends whom they honor. Equally few and far scattered are those who yearn for good advice.

So, unless officially, as by right of being

a tutor, or an employer, or a parent, a husband or a wife, be chary of saying to any one, "You are unwise in this movement, you are foolishly investing your time and your strength ; you are spending too much money." And do not, as you value your peace of mind, interfere between relatives, which is to put your fingers between the bark and the tree.

Virginia Van de Water tells us that, "There is a time-worn phrase which warns us that it is a dangerous matter to put a finger between the bark and the tree. Like many adages, this is so old that we seldom pause to consider the truth and wisdom it contains. There are in life many relations that are as close and natural as that of the bark and the tree. Husband and wife, brother and sister, parent and child, are connected by a bond with which the stranger intermeddleth not ; or if he is so unwary as to intermeddle, a pinched finger is almost sure to be the result of his interference. Few of us will tolerate the most well-meant suggestion with regard to the proper behavior of those we love. A case in point was brought to my notice a few days ago. A sister was sadly disappointed at the betrothal of a favorite brother to a girl who, while perfectly good and decidedly pretty, was absolutely unintellectual and uninteresting. She expressed her disappointment at George's choice to a near friend. The friend, with the best in-

tentions in the world, sympathized after
this fashion,—

" ' I am so sorry that George has made
such a choice.  It is too bad !  After all you
have done for that boy I should think he
would have some consideration for you.   I
call it ingratitude and abominable selfishness on his part.'

"Whereat the lately disappointed sister
veered about with a rapidity that amazed
her listener.

" ' Ingratitude and selfishness !   It is
nothing of the kind ; for there was never a
more thoughtful or considerate brother than
George has always been.   And as to his
future wife—*he* is to marry her, and has
chosen her because he loves her.   I really
suppose even I have no right to be disappointed.  He is satisfied, and that is enough.'

"The person accustomed to the vagaries of
mankind will, if taken into the family secrets
of his friend, be careful to sympathize cau-
tiously, praise diplomatically, and refrain
from all censure.   A wife may be so far forgetful of self-respect and honor as to complain of her husband.   Her listener, while
pitying her, must not express dislike or disapproval of the recreant spouse, unless she
would bring down upon her the wrath of
the abused wife.   To do man justice, he seldom discusses with his most intimate friend
the foibles of his wife.   In this matter his
sense of honor is perhaps finer than that of

the average woman. But if a husband forgets the traditions of his class and confides his conjugal infelicities to some acquaintance, let her beware of how she accepts this confidence. Unless the disagreement is so serious as to lead to open separation or divorce, the husband is certain to swing back to his allegiance to his wife, the keeper of his home and the mother of his children. And in the self-disgust following upon his return to his normal condition, he will hate the indiscreet friend who allowed him to speak unkindly of the best woman in the world.

"We cannot snub the acquaintance who brings us her complaint against husband, brother, sister, or parent. But we can refrain from criticism or the utterance of a decided opinion. When one is placed in this awkward position she must needs have the wisdom of the serpent and the seeming guilelessness of the dove.

"The bark clings to the tree in spite of the meddling and officious poking and prying of weak fingers. These pull at the bark until it seems to yield a little, but it springs back with a force and suddenness that abrade the flesh and start the blood. A tremendous effort may tear all the bark from the parent trunk, in which case the tree, bereft of the close and natural protection, will probably die."

It is a homely adage, brusque and terse,

and not usually sounded in ears polite, but there is golden wit and good sense in the words "Mind your own business!" For, if you do mind it seriously and constantly you will know when and of whom and in what manner to seek advice and when you receive it you will value it at its true worth.

In some relations we not only seek advice but pay generously to have it given, as when we ask the doctor to come to our relief and are willing to pay his fee over and over for the sake of the service he does us. We pay for suggestions from those who know more than we do in certain fields of science; we are glad to be legally counselled when our property is threatened, or a boundary line is to be settled, or there comes a question of deeds and titles. When advice is a matter of business interest, it is wholly unlike gratuitous advice, which if you would be loved and esteemed you would better keep strictly to yourself.

## MEN, WOMEN, AND SOCIETY.

Whether or not we care very much about society depends largely on our degree of animal spirits.   A perfectly healthy, well-balanced mind does not avoid its fellows. When people desire to live as hermits and recluses, it is an indication that they are not quite well in every respect.

The Bible word "Thou shalt be made whole," in reference to health, is very suggestive.   At the same time it must be admitted that many excellent people of domestic tastes prefer their own homes and their own circles to a larger group of friends outside.   Mr. Junius Henri Browne, writing on this subject, says in an article published in *Harper's Bazar :*—

It may seem strange to doubt that men enjoy society, when it could not exist without them, and when they always form part of it.   But this may very well be without any enjoyment on their side.   While many men doubtless like society, the bulk of them do not,  and frankly acknowledge the fact, though not, of course, to their host or hostess, which would be an unpardonable rudeness.   We are all compelled by social laws to suppress truth sometimes ; politeness being held by them as paramount to everything else. If men dislike society, why do they go into it? may naturally be asked.

They go into it because their sweethearts, sisters, wives, all their feminine kindred and friends go, and are determined that they shall go too.

What woman wills in regard to the other sex, she is apt to carry out ; what she greatly wants she is apt to get. And she certainly wills and earnestly wants that men shall perform their share in society by frequenting it when she does, and by appearing in company with her. This fully explains and reconciles their incongruity.

Nearly all men, husbands particularly, know how energetically and continually they are importuned on that subject. It is useless for them to declare society in general a supreme bore ; that they hate it, and hate it more and more, the more they see of it ; that it is an intolerable nuisance, with similar extravagances to which we men are prone when badgered about anything. Woman understands perfectly how to deal with such cases ; she is used to them ; however violent, they disturb not her a bit. In the first place, she does not believe that we speak the exact truth on that topic ; that we grossly exaggerate at least ; that we cannot feel what we say. Naturally enough. She is so fond of society herself, and whatever per-

tains to it, that she cannot regard it as tire-
some, as positively disagreeable.  She is sure
that there is a mistake somewhere.  It is
always very hard for her to think anything
unpleasant which she regards as pleasant, or
to have any of her favorite opinions contro-
verted.  Besides, society is, to her, a change,
a relief, a recreation, unless she has an
excess of it.  She cannot comprehend why
we should find it the reverse of these ; and
she is confident that two  or three hours
passed in somebody else's drawing-room,
with lights and flowers, conversation and
refreshments, music and gay company, will
refresh and delight us.  It ought to perhaps ;
but does it ?

Woman often contends that going into
society is a duty, which men will not admit,
unless it be a duty to be bored.  She maintains that they have no right to be bored by
it, and they would not be if they were constituted as they should be.  This kind of argument, especially feminine, is difficult to
meet.  She also holds that for men to go out
frequently, regularly during the season, is an
obligation to her personally and to the sex ;
that they who do not go out cannot esteem,
appreciate, or even care for women.

Men laugh at this idea ; deny it stoutly ;
assert that meeting women socially tends to
create a prejudice against them rather than
in their favor.  Women, it is claimed, appear to disadvantage in society ; are never

seen at their best ; lose there much of their
fine quality and individual charm. They
are of directly opposite opinion, considering
themselves most attractive, most dangerous
to masculine peace, when in elaborately
dressed,elegant, brilliant company. As they
assuredly try then to appear at their very
best, they naturally think that they do so
appear. But may not the extraordinary
effort they make interfere with their object ?
Are they not most interesting, most winning
when free from any ambition to shine, when
in comparative repose, when least conscious
of themselves ?

There is scarcely a rational doubt that the
sexes differ radically about the allurements
of society. It is almost as rare to find a
man who enjoys it for its own sake as to
find a woman who does not. He can no
more tell why she likes it, than she can tell
why he dislikes it ; and, as we have seen,
she cannot be convinced that his dislike
is sincere. She catechizes him closely ; she
labors hard to get at the significance of
his objections ; she is anxious to expose his
fallacies. She is inclined to maintain, as a
general proposition, that a man that hates
society hates women who are devoted to it ;
who are its keepers and guardians, its inspir-
ing element, its very soul. Of course he will
not agree to that. He holds the deduction to
be wholly illogical, as it evidently is. While
the majority of men would unquestionably

keep out of society, in its conventional sense, if they were let alone, if they were allowed to have their own way, they could scarcely be prevailed on to keep away from woman, to whom they gravitate by nature's law.

Dr. Holland, who had a way of getting at the bottom of things which few men of our time have surpassed, speaks of the dislike of certain people for society as existing very widely among students and thoughtful men. He says that those who confine themselves within doors and exhaust their nervous energy in thought and composition, receiving no vigor from the open air, are necessarily without an overflow of spirits. In other words, they have lost the disposition to play.

We find this in hard-working men whose energies are absorbed by business, in farmers, whose toil is all day monotonous and irksome, bowing the back and taking from the mind the elasticity which it once had. If you have ever noticed in reading memoirs of men who have been largely in the public eye, the first volume is full of exhilaration, hope and ecstasy ; but the second volume, when the men have grown middle-aged and sadder, has none of that overflowing vitality, and is often more largely a record of home life and solitary musing than of a blithe and bright going to and fro.

So we find the gay girl. After she marries and the burden of motherhood comes upon her, she becomes careless of society, not seeking it any more or striving to make herself happy in it. Then, too, there are people who do not know quite how to act in certain circumstances. They find themselves, from having stayed too much at home and from having lived largely out of the world, ill at ease and strangers when they come into a social circle.

If these good people would only accept my word for it, they would believe that there is no great art after all in practising the requisite conventionalities. You go to a house, you speak to your hostess, you look interested, you answer what is said to you, you observe what is going on, and you come away, always remembering to take a kind leave of your entertainer, and that is all there is about it.

No one can fail to receive benefit from going into society more or less, and if we do not wish to become fossils we must come out from our shelves, accept invitations, and mingle with our kind. To quote from Dr. Holland again :

" You must contrive some scheme for meeting society half-way. You are unlike most men who shun society if you do not feel that it does not quite do its duty to you, in not coming after you. You retire into yourself, you take no pains to show that you possess the slightest social value, you do not even exhibit that interest in humanity generally, or in the community in which you live, that leads you to efforts on their behalf, yet, somehow, you feel that society ought to find you out, and bring you out, and make itself agreeable and valuable to you. You may rest assured that society will never do any such thing. I know that you have no native impulse to social communion —that the spirit of play about which I have talked is gone out of you even if you ever possessed it—but that which most men do by impulse or natural desire, you must do by direct purpose, and as a matter of duty. And you must do this at once. The penalty of failure is the gradual dwarfing of yourself and the sacrifice of all power to influence others. You have a laudable desire to be something and to do something in the world, and know that you have within you the ability necessary to accomplish your purposes, but without social sympathy, you will never know what to do, or how to do for the world, and the world will find it impossible to understand and receive you."

Society is ideally excellent and admirable when it includes people of all ages. If it is made up wholly of the young it is crude and unsatisfying ; if it is made up wholly of the old it settles down into a very slow-going, unprogressive affair.

Youth and age must continually meet. There must be a common ground where they can mingle, and this can be found nowhere

better than in the drawing-room, where
charming people of all ages come together
on an equal plane.

One of the pleasantest evenings I ever
spent was in the home of a friend, whose
mother, a beautiful woman past her eighti-
eth year, received the guests most graciously, every one who had a smile and a
word from her feeling as if he or she had been
especially blessed.

The daughter, a gracious and elegant
woman, unmarried, not because she had not
been sought, but for the reason that she
preferred her own independence, gathered
about her a company of men and women,
some noted in art, others distinguished in
literature, still other gay girls just introduced
to society, and young men at home from
college on their vacations.

There were games, in which we all took
part.   There was much delightful conversation.   We had a little music.   We had a
supper which the girls cooked and the men
served.   It was just before Christmas, and
a little stocking was hung up in the chimney
corner for every guest.   We had conun-
drums, enigmas, and all sorts of merry jests,
and before we parted we all sang a lovely
good-night hymn.

Seldom in any home have I witnessed
anything more beautiful and more distinc-
tive than this little company; and the glory
of it all was the dear mother who sat in her

13

corner of the sofa like a queen upon her throne. When society is most agreeable and gives us of its best, we may always expect to find in it men and women of all ages from eighteen to eighty.

## GROWN–UP SONS AND DAUGHTERS.

There comes a point in life when people drop childhood and find themselves face to face with the problems and difficulties of life. Every one of us has to live life for ourselves ; no one can take our place or do our work. Fathers are apt to forget that sons reach an hour when they must be allowed to choose their own paths, and mothers often are the last to realize that the little girl whom they have loved in the nursery and guarded so carefully through her childhood is now herself a woman.

When it comes to choosing a career, let the parents advise wisely, but let them beware of forcing upon the children a lot in life which will not be for the child's advantage or pleasure. In the old days a daughter never thought of making a home for herself away from her parents' roof, unless she married and went to the house of her husband. Nothing is now more common than for a young woman who has acquired a profession or art, and is self-supporting, to desire a home of her own, perhaps in conjunction with several friends.

I do not like the phrase "bachelor girl,"

and prefer the old-fashioned "spinster" as descriptive of the single woman ; and in the little spinster homes of which I know—cozy apartments where women make a nest for themselves, and where they have their own background, whence they go forth to their work—I have seen some of the sweetest home life of which I have any knowledge.

If a girl arrives at a point when she cannot possibly be happy at home, when the restraints of home are irksome, and she longs for independence and a career, by all means, provided she has reached maturity, by which I do not mean any age under thirty, let her pitch her tent for herself.

If a son is thoroughly unfit for his father's business and longs for an artistic career, let him be gratified if possible. There are too many misfits in life, and this is at the root of a great deal of life's discontent. The person who defined happiness as satisfaction with one's environment was not very far wrong.

When we see the man who ought to be driving a plough attempting to fill a place in the pulpit, or the mechanic wearily plodding on in the law, or any other evident failure among our friends, we may not always know the reasons which have led to the state of things, but they lie quite often in mistaken ambition.

One of the questions usually asked a boy when he is growing up is, "What are you

going to be?" It is not possible for a boy or
girl in the period of adolescence to know
just what life they will lead, but we may
set it down as a maxim that parents should
let grown-up sons and daughters choose
their own course and manage their lives, as
far as possible, to please themselves. Authority ceases with the necessity for constant protection, yet we have known middle-aged women and men who still sought
in all things parental guidance and counsel.
This is entirely as it should be, but there
should not be anything like dictation after
maturity is reached.

Especially are parents apt to meddle in
the love affairs of grown-up sons and daughters. One hears again and again the old
complaint, "I am weary of my life because
of the daughters of Heth." What! can it be
that the boy who has been the idol of the
mother's heart through all the early years is
about to throw himself away on a girl who
to the mother's eyes is more than commonplace, when "He might have," she proudly
thinks, "chosen his pick from all the women
in the land!"

The more she frets, the more she opposes,
the more she is disturbed about the choice,
probably the stronger will be the bond
which loyalty and affection will weave
about the girl, whom the young man clings
to all the more steadfastly that his people do
not care for her.

Surely, if one ever has a right to exercise one's own prerogative, it is in the selection of a comrade for life ; and yet children would do well to trust the love which has been theirs during life's storms and sunshine, and at least not to act in haste or upon impulse. Where there is opposition, it is not a bad plan to delay for a little the consummation of the engagement. No great harm can be done by a period of waiting, during which the young people may become better acquainted, while the older ones may withdraw their opposition.

The young man and the young woman, coming from different families and forming a new home, will naturally find themselves under a fire of criticism, and it is quite likely that the relations-in-law on both sides may not entirely approve of the new connection, but, if there be true love, after a while everything will adjust itself.

Rev. James C. Fernald says, "The coming of true love changes the whole life of a young man, his best earnings and his earliest savings often beginning from that time. It is astonishing how those imprudent marriages so often turn out well, where the worthy youth and maiden, with no capital but their hands and brains and knowledge of honest work and love for one another, sail out together on life's ocean in life's springtime."

It is to be doubted if any man has ever

greatly influenced the world for good who
has not had back of all achievements the
deep, pure love of woman—mother, sister,
wife, or perhaps the wife that might have
been. Woman's wealth of affection makes
her often a wonderful helper in ways that
would have been least expected. In emergencies there will be found none wiser in
counsel nor readier in resource than a sensible mother or wife. Her love is stronger than
death. The man's heart harboring it says,
"There is goodness and hope in the world
and in me so long as such love is possible
for me, and every noble energy in me rises
up to be worthy of that one pure and noble
affection."

When fathers and mothers have any mer-
cenary reason, or, because they have looked
higher for their children, object to the course
of true love, they are putting an obstacle in
the path of Divine Providence, and are in-
curring a very great danger. There is first
the danger of alienation,

" The little rift within the lute
    That by and by may make the music mute."

There is next the peril that even if recon-
ciliation comes there will always be the
memory of the wound—some wounds leave
deep scars. The pitcher that is mended
may stand on the shelf, but it can never
again go to the well. In our home life we
need, of all things, to guard against quarrels

and recrimination, and disagreeable words
and looks which may linger and haunt us
to our dying day.

In another chapter we have referred to
the Gurneys of Earlham. One of the
sisters of this family, Richenda, married a
clergyman and became Mrs. Cunningham.
She possessed a wonderful power for at-
tracting young people to her. Of her home
it was said, ''No other place is like it in its
freedom, its wonderful activity, its thoughtful kindness, and its truly parental care
over everybody. Everything was marked
by generosity and truest charity. Not only
nieces and nephews were welcome here,
but the Cunninghams made so sunshiny a
house for themselves that all young people
rejoiced to be with them, and in a sense
they were parents to those not of their own
flesh and blood.'' Some of us have met
people who have this beautiful gift of at-
tracting to them those to whom their personality is in itself a benediction.

Every home should widen itself out sufficiently to include at times in its merry-makings and in its ordinary course the friends
of its children. Nothing is more pleasant
than to see a house filled to the overflow
with young people, the boys and girls freely
bringing their friends to their parents' table
and to the family gatherings.

This can never be possible in homes
where the parents lose touch with their

children. No other thing keeps us so young
as sympathy with the young, and as parents
and children go together hand in hand
through the years, they are making for
themselves a wealth of associations which
will dignify and delight every year of their
lives.

One sometimes sees instances in which
children who have had better education and
advantages than their parents are desirous of
keeping the latter in the background. There
has been something radically wrong in home
training which can permit such a thing as
this. The most disgreeable sight in the
world is a daughter ashamed of or apologetic
for her father and mother, or a son who
seeks to hide the plainness of the family
life from which he sprang.

Some years ago while visiting in a Southern town quite back from the railroad, I
found myself the kind object of solicitude
on the part of some of the townspeople,
who were good enough to call. One day
I received a call from two beautiful young
ladies, who were profuse in their kind invitations and offers to show me all the
beauties of the place. A few days later I
returned their visit.

While seated in the drawing-room, where
the open windows gave a view of the lawn
and a glimpse of well-kept flower-beds, I
noticed hovering in the dim distance of the
back parlor a little quaint old lady, who

wavered back and forth like a timid shadow.
She evidently wished to come in, but did
not like to advance into the room where her
daughters and their guest were, and although
once or twice she came almost to the
middle of the room, no encouragement was
given by the girls to approach nearer.

Although I said nothing, I suppose my
face revealed my thoughts and my solicitude
about this old lady, for presently one of the
young women smiled and said, "You need
not mind mother ; we never ask her to come
in when we have company." Evidently
they wanted to keep their poor mother out
of sight, and my opinion of them sank very
low from that moment.

Most people have sufficient tact to refrain
from showing so plainly a weakness of this
kind, but where one finds in any family one
member ashamed of another, one may
be sure that there has been at some time
or other a great lack in the home atmosphere and a great want in the home
training.

Our whole land has rejoiced when, as it
has happened more than once, a man of the
people has been raised to the highest station. Such men as Lincoln, Garfield and
McKinley, to say nothing of others less con-
spicuous, confer an honor upon us by the
recognition which they have given of the
home training and love which have been
about them always. The manner in which

they have shown honor to their mothers has won the true regard of all the people.

We may be sure that when sons and daughters come to great distinction that the mother who bore them and the father who was their earliest example have had good sense all the way, not only in childhood but afterward. The mother of Frances Willard said to her one day, when the gifted younger woman was hesitating about entering on some work which had offered itself, "My daughter, when God opens a door for you, never hesitate about walking through it." Such mothers do not hold their children back; they urge them forward, and they share whatever triumphs come to the younger generation.

## TACT.

Tact means touch.   When we are in touch
with people we understand that we have a
peculiar sympathy, that there is a thrill which
goes from heart to heart and from hand to
hand.   When we are not in touch with
people, they jar upon us, and we are unhappy in their company.   When we are
truly in touch with a friend we may sit in
that friend's house in perfect silence and an
hour may pass in which we say no word
and hear nothing, but the friend knows and
we know that everything is all right.

Tact in society is that fine delicacy of
feeling which keeps us from making blunders
and which sets everyone at ease.   To some
extent tact is innate.   There are people
highly gifted with this quality ; others acquire it by the exercise of thought and care.

The tactful person does not say the wrong
thing at the wrong moment.   If the tactful
person pays a compliment it is suited to the
person and the occasion ; and in fact tact is
the oil upon the waters which keeps everything in society smooth and peaceful.

I suppose you have heard that in a literal
way oil poured upon the ocean waves will

calm them when they are in great agitation. Steamers going to sea sometimes carry with them profusion of oil, to be used in case of a tempest, and as they pour it out upon the perturbed waves, they become calm and still. So often there is need that oil should be gently poured on the agitated waters of life.

Who has not at a breakfast table heard a querulous word or observed how quickly and with what sweet and loving tact the mother turns it aside? Who has not known in certain circles how beloved and welcome is the young girl or the young man who always may be depended upon for smoothing out difficulties and making everything move pleasantly along?

In the old fairy tales there were spiteful elves who delighted in setting tasks which were hard to do, such as giving a poor princess a heap of feathers of all kinds which were to be sorted and set in order, or a great tangle of silks to unwind or some other equally difficult task to perform; and then very often there would come in the good fairy, who, with a little touch here and a little touch there would set all the feathers in the places where they belonged, unravel the tangled heaps of silk, finish the work which was so hard, and presently let the prisoner go smiling forth with everything done which she had been set to do.

The good fairy in modern life is tact. Tact

does not feel called upon ever to say a disagreeable thing.   Is tact therefore insincere,
and must we say that the tactful person is
of necessity untrue?   There is an erroneous
opinion abroad to this effect, and we sometimes hear people say, "Oh, I am a plain,
outspoken sort of woman ; I always speak
my mind with great frankness.   You may
know where to find me ; I always say what
I think."

Dear lady, you have no right on all occasions to say just what you think ; it is often
the better plan to keep your thoughts very
much to yourself.   Make it your rule in life
never needlessly to say an unpleasant thing ;
say a sweet and bright thing if you can truly
do so and leave the others aside.

There is a sort of candor which is mere
brutality and which cannot be justified by
any canon of human law, and on which we
are sure the dear Lord does not smile.   I am
not called upon to comment on the defects
of my friends.   It may be my duty to my
own children, in privacy, and with great
care not needlessly to wound their feelings,
to tell them of something I see in them that
is wrong and may be amended ; but as a
rule it is wise not to go through the world
telling people of their faults.

The tactful mistress does not reprove her
maids before anyone.   The tactful wife
passes over the little friction, the moment-
ary irritation, which another would have

noticed and which would have produced a
breeze, if not a gale, in the house. The tactful friend finding his friend a little blue and
out of sorts does not comment upon it, but
calls attention to some pleasant thing.

Better than beauty, better than jewels,
better than any other gift of which we know
is the blessed gift of tact, which lightens all
drudgery, makes home delightful, and fills
the social hour and the drawing-room with
a charm beyond the power of words to express. Of the tactful person it may be said,

> She doth little kindnesses
> Which most leave undone or despise,
> For naught that sets one's heart at ease,
> Or giveth happiness or peace,
> Is low esteemed in her eyes.

One reason among others why it is pleasant for young people to have a chaperon
when they go on merry-makings and excursions, as is now the custom among all well-
bred people, is that an older woman has
tact and can meet emergencies as young
girls cannot be expected to. Time was
when in the newness of our country great
freedom was allowed in the intercourse of
the sexes, and young men and maidens
scorned the idea of a duenna, or of any over-
sight from parents and friends.

We have advanced far enough now to
understand that it is always safer and pleas-
anter not to be separated into herds of young
and old, but for the younger and the older to

mix up and have their pleasures in common.
Superior age and a longer experience, with
greater knowledge of human nature, enables
the older woman or the woman who is married to know just what to do and say on
occasions which might prove embarrassing
to younger people.

To do our American young people justice,
they have usually a good deal of self-respect
and of common sense. I think they may
be trusted to do the right thing in most
cases, but in our large cities, where we have
a shifting foreign population, where people
have come from the old world with low
ideals of womanhood, where it is possible
that a young, pure girl away from her
mother's wing may receive insult and not
know just how to meet it, there is a certain
measure of safety in being accompanied by
mother or aunt or some friendly older person
when on a journey. At the same time,
where there is no chaperon let the young
girl act with so much discretion that none
will be necessary.

Tact is perhaps more purely a feminine
than a masculine quality. Women have
more finesse, are apt to understand a situation more quickly, and do not need to have
everything told outright as men do. We
see this even in boys and girls. Teachers
will tell you that the faults of boys are more
on the surface, that they are more direct in
everything than girls are, and that girls are

a little harder to manage because they are more susceptible to emotion and have little reserves and concealments which are not possible to their brothers.

We must not confound tact with insincerity, and yet the one danger to which the tactful person is exposed is that sometimes, in the desire to avoid giving offence and in the well-meant intention to keep everything smooth and happy, she may perhaps infringe upon the exact truth.

Of all the tactful and bewitching people, the one who wins my heart beyond any other is the dear, manly boy who has had a mother's training, and who goes through the home thoughtfully, though merrily, whose whole life is a beautiful thing because it is so cheery and so sweet. Of such a boy, years ago, I wrote the verses which follow :

> I knew him for a gentleman
>   By signs that never fail;
> His coat was rough and rather worn,
>   His cheeks were thin and pale—
> A lad who had his way to make.
>   With little time to play ;
> I knew him for a gentleman
>   By certain signs to-day.
>
> He met his mother on the street ;
>   Off came his little cap.
> My door was shut ; he waited there
>   Until I heard his rap.
> He took the bundle from my hand,
>   And when I dropped my pen
> He sprang to pick it up for me—
>   This gentleman of ten.

He does not push and crowd along;
　His voice is gently pitched;
He does not fling his books about
　As if he were bewitched.
He stands aside to let you pass;
　He always shuts the door;
He runs on errands willingly
　To forge and mill and store.

He thinks of you before himself,
　He serves you if he can;
For, in whatever company,
　The manners make the man.
At ten or forty, 'tis the same:
　The manner tells the tale,
And I discern the gentleman
　By signs that never fail.

## PURITY OF SPEECH.

It is so easy to drop into the use of slang, and so much is our speech a matter of imitation, that many of us fail to speak with the purity which we admire. There are certain objectionable forms which one hears from people who know very much better, as, for example, when a person tells you that "Mrs. Hamilton invited Robert and I to dine with her last night." It should have been, of course, "Robert and me."

People from whom you do not expect such slipshod English say, "He hadn't ought to have done this or that," and such forms as "ain't" and "don't." "Don't" being used with the singular nominative; "ain't" being wholly inexusable, are so frequently heard, from children particularly, that one wonders where the schoolmaster can be.

Many people have a way of using foolish exclamations, such as "Great Scott!" and "By Jove." Others, sliding rapidly downhill, introduce into their ordinary talk forms which are almost profane. In my youth I was taught that all such expressions as "goodness" and "mercy" were touching upon the attributes of God, and should not

be used in common conversation.   All sorts
of slang, such as "You make me tired,"
"It is too thin," and the like, are violations
of purity of speech.

A writer in the *The Outlook*, speaking of
this subject, remarks that it is by training
the observing faculty that we accomplish
wonders in the education of our children.

A lady was talking with a bright, clever
girl, who at school had made a study of
words and prided herself on her freedom
from the use of slipshod English.   The lady
said, "What a strange expression that is,
'thinks, says I.'"   "Why," said the young
girl, "I never heard it ; it is an impossible
expression."

The lady did not say "Why, you your-
self sometimes use it," but she said, "Listen
to others, and then tell me what you think."
I was told that the next day the young girl
came to her kind critic and said, "Mrs.
Blank, I not only heard Edythe Parks say
'Thinks, says I,' but I heard myself say it.
I was so surprised."

A boy of ten was playing with a boy of
seven, whose mother did not think him
physically strong enough to bear the stimulating atmosphere of school life.   Finally,
the boy of ten began to crow over the boy
of seven, saying, "Funny you can't spell
that word in that book !  You had ought to
go to school.   It ain't a hard word to spell.
Why, I can spell enough sight harder words

'an that. I wish you could hear 'um. I study gography an' grammer. You don't know nothing 'bout 'rithmetic, I 'spose. You wasn't ever at school." And so on. I heard many expressions which were far from being good English.

It is not because we do not know better that we make mistakes : it is simply for the reason that we are careless and that we suffer in ourselves the use of language which a little thought would keep us from falling into.

We should talk less and say more, and be less frivolous in our conversation if we made it a rule to think before speaking, instead of afterwards. If two shorthand writers, placed behind a curtain, were to take down the conversation at a single afternoon tea, and publish it in the newspaper next morning, the talkers would see with shame an illustration of the truth of Pope's lines—

" Words are like leaves ; and where they most abound
Much fruit of sense beneath is rarely found."

It is recorded of good old Latimer, that, when examined before Bonner, at first he answered without much thought and care ; but presently, hearing the rustling of a pen behind the curtain, he perceived that they were taking down every word of his defence. Stopping, he thus apostrophized himself ; "Oh Latimer, Latimer ! thy words are being put on record. Thou must take heed what thou art saying!"

In certain parts of our country it is customary for people to drop the final "g." They say "mornin'" and "evenin'". Our vocabularies are limited because we do not read enough. The habit of reading good books forms in us a habit of seeing and mentally hearing the best language.

Perhaps many persons have had their ordinary speech somewhat vitiated by too much reading of realistic stories, written colloquially and in dialect. Formerly people were more stately, and one seldom heard the lapses among educated people which one hears now.

Every one should determine to be familiar with some of the best books. She will find, with Macaulay, that "Books are better than all the tarts and cakes, toys and plays, and sights in the world. If anybody would make me the greatest king that ever lived, with palaces and gardens and fine dinners, and wine and coaches and beautiful clothes and hundreds of servants, on condition that I would not read books, I would not be a king. I would rather be a poor man in a garret with plenty of books than a king who did not love reading."

In "Sesame and Lilies," Ruskin says:

"Now, in order to deal with words rightly, this is the habit you must form. Nearly every word in your language has been first

a word of some other language—of Saxon,
German, French, Latin, or Greek (not to
speak of eastern and primitive dialects).
And many words have been all these ;—that
is to say, have been Greek first, Latin next,
French or German next, and English last ;
undergoing a certain change of sense and
use on the lips of each nation ; but retain-
ing a deep vital meaning which all good
scholars feel in employing them, even at
this day. If you do not know the Greek
alphabet, learn it ; young or old—girl or
boy—whoever you may be, if you think of
reading seriously (which, of course, implies
that you have some leisure at command), 
learn your Greek alphabet ; then get good
dictionaries of all these languages, and whenever you are in doubt about a word, hunt
it down patiently. Read Max Müller's
lectures thoroughly, to begin with ; and,
after that, never let a word escape you that
looks suspicious. It is severe work ; but
you will find it, even at first, interesting,
and at last, endlessly amusing. And the
general gain to your character, in power
and precision, will be quite incalculable.

" Mind, this does not imply knowing, or
trying to know, Greek, or Latin, or French.
It takes a whole life to learn any language
perfectly. But you can easily ascertain the
meanings through which the English word
has passed ; and those which in a good
writer's work it must still bear."

He adds, "We make the worst possible use of our opportunities if we allow mere books of the hour to usurp the place of true books : for, strictly speaking, they are not books at all, but merely letters or newspapers in good print. Our friend's letter may be delightful, or necessary, to-day : whether worth keeping or not, is to be considered. The newspaper may be entirely proper at breakfast time, but assuredly it is not reading for all day. So, though bound up in a volume, the long letter which gives you so pleasant an account of the inns, and roads, and weather last year at such a place, or which tells you that amusing story, or gives you the real circumstances of such and such events, however valuable for occasional reference, may not be, in the real sense of the word, a "book" at all, nor, in the real sense, to be "read." A book is essentially not a talked thing, but a written thing ; and written, not with the view of mere communication, but of permanence. The book of talk is printed only because its author cannot speak to thousands of people at once ; if he could, he would—the volume is mere *multiplication* of his voice. You cannot talk to your friend in India ; if you could, you would ; you write instead : that is mere *conveyance* of voice. But a book is written, not to multiply the voice merely, not to carry it merely, but to preserve it. The author has something to say which he perceives to be true and useful, or helpfully beautiful. So far as he knows, no one has yet said it ; so far as he knows, no one else can say it.

Ian Maclaren remarks, in one of his lectures in "A Cure of Souls," that clergymen should use simple words in their sermons, but also that they should occasionally use a beautiful word, which is like embroidery upon their style. He remarks that people acquire something of their style of speech from the sermons they habitually hear.

I was reminded of this not long ago in a public conveyance, where I heard two workingmen discussing the merits of an orator to whom they had listened. One said, "He speaks very well ; he uses straight, short words which anybody can understand." "But," said the other, "I like better to hear a man who has long, fine words which sound like a trumpet."

It seems to me that the truth lay between the two men, and that we need in our common speech the best words we can find to convey our thought—sometimes the grand and sonorous, sometimes the simple and plain ; but we shall never be attractive if our ordinary speech is impure or if we violate our obligation to be respectful to the English tongue in which we were born.

## DEFERENCE TO THE OLD.

The Seminole Indians, of whom a little remnant remains in Florida, have a beautiful way of treating the aged among them, a way which we, more enlightened and civilized than the Seminoles, might well emulate. When in the little remnant of their tribe there is found a very old man or woman whose children and grandchildren perhaps have died, this person is treated as the most distinguished member of the tribe.

He spends three months at a time as the guest of each family. While there he is treated with great distinction, the warmest corner by the fire, the best chair, the best food, and the best bed are given to him. The young people vie with each other in administering to his wants, and when the time comes that one visit is completed, he is escorted to the next house and received there as if he were a prince whose visit conferred a great favor upon the house to which he comes.

Too often we forget to be deferential to the old. We grow impatient with the exactions of old people, forgetting that they are living in a lonely world, that those who

were young with them have passed away,
and that the ranks of their friends have
grown thin ; that it may be there is no one
remaining who knew them in childhood's
day, and who calls them by the familiar pet
name which was once theirs. They have
ceased to be Ed and Jack and Dick, they
are Mr. So-and-So; and while they live
largely in the past, too often our pushing,
present-day people have no time to spend
with them.

Some years ago in a little town in Massa-
chusetts one summer day a very old woman was found drowned in a brook. The
brook was so shallow that the poor old
creature had been obliged to lie face down-
ward in the water in order to put an end
to the life of which she was so tired that
her mind had given way beneath the
strain.

I was told that she lived in a family of
relatives where they were good to her in all
material ways, but where they had very
little patience with her ; where, in fact, they
grew tired of her meanderings over the past,
where the daughters and granddaughters
refused to let her take any share in the work
of the house, and where she felt herself
continually an incumbrance. At last life
was too much for her, and slipping away
when the family were at a picnic and she
was left alone at home, she went to the little
brook. laid down there and died.

There is surely some great fault when old people are permitted to feel themselves thus neglected. A more beautiful quality than that of reverence cannot be found, and that our young people are largely deficient in this is a great pity and speaks badly for their bringing up. We need to cultivate the habit of deference to those older than ourselves, deference to their opinions, deference to their wishes, considerateness about their comfort.

In the beautiful idyl of Ruth and Naomi, than which nothing more tender and beautiful can be found in literature, we see the desolate old woman—husband gone, sons gone—turning her face back to the home she had left years before. Her daughters-in-law, Ruth and Orpah, go with her to the hillside which bounds the land of Moab, that they may take leave of her. At the last moment Orpah kisses her mother-in-law and leaves her, but Ruth refuses to be separated from the old, yet beloved, woman, into whose home she had come as the bride of Naomi's son.

She says : "Entreat me not to leave thee, nor to return from following after thee, for whither thou goest I will go, where thou lodgest I will lodge, where thou diest I will die, and there will I be buried. God do so to me, and more also, if aught but death part thee and me." And so it has come to pass that, glistening like a gem in the canon of sacred Scripture, we find the immortal story of Ruth.

Longfellow says, in one of his beautiful lyrics,—

> "Long was the good man's sermon,
>   But it seemed not so to me ;
>   For I thought of Ruth, the beautiful,
>   And then I thought of thee."

And one of the sweetest pictures we possess anywhere in the annals of pastoral love is that of Ruth gleaning amid the alien corn. It is because she clung to age and weakness that she lives forever on the canvas of the sacred historian.

We notice how cheerfully Ruth takes upon herself the management of their small house-keeping, after she and Naomi arrive at Beth-lehem, how she imparts to the older woman that she shall go out with the maidens and glean after the reapers, and how tenderly and deferentially she yields to the counsel of Naomi. Then later, when she marries Boaz and her child is born, it is to Naomi that they bring the little one, and holding this dear baby in her arms, Naomi is com-forted for all she has lost.

I found the other day a tender little story about one who had been waiting a long time to go home to the dear one who had left her :

"'Don't set down in that chair, dearie. Yer gran'pa'll be in pretty soon, an' he'll be tired after doin' all the chores.'

" The child, with a look of pity on her small, bright face, slipped out of the chair and ran in the pantry to her mother. 'Say, ma, she thinks he's comin' again to-night, an' she's fixin' the chair.'

" 'Well, dear, don't notice it; the fancy don't seem to do her any harm as I see.'

" Grandma drew the armchair a little nearer to her own, and smoothed out and patted the cushion over and over.

" 'Yer gran'pa'll be tired an' cold; he's been out a good spell, an' he's lame. He allers is when the wind blows. It 'pears to take him a long time to do the chores. Sometimes I think mebbe he ain't so spry as he use to be; but I reckon he'll be in in a minnit.'

" She patted the cushion a little more, and then folding her handkerchief back and forth, she hummed a soft, quaint melody. Nearly four years had passed since her dear old husband had sat in his familiar place, but she lived in a sort of placid dream, not realizing the lapse of time, or grieving. Only when the wind blew hard enough to attract her attention she grew restless, dropping many stitches in her knitting; and as twilight came on she fancied he was out around the barns, and would soon be in, cold and weary.

" She did not suffer from disappointment, for lights and supper mercifully made her forget how sad and fruitless was her wait-

ing, and how long. But one March afternoon a furious storm was raging, and the
wind came in rushes that made the house
tremble. Grandma put aside her beloved
knitting, which had so many ravelling
stitches in it, and began earlier than usual
to fix the chair and pat the cushion.

" ' Yer gran'pa'll sartinly be chilled through
doin' the chores to-night,' she said, in troubled, quavering tones. ' I do hope he'll be
along in soon.'

" The clouds settled down dark and heavy,
and twilight came suddenly. ' Why, Wes-
ley, I've been a-waitin' so long !' The
voice rang out glad and clear. They
brought lights hastily. Grandma was lean-
ing back among her cushions, breathless
and white, with a welcoming smile on her
dear, sweet face."

Of one thing we may all be sure. We
will never regret, or for a moment be sorry
for, any kindness we have shown to the old.
Little by little, with soft, imperceptible
touches, the years are stealing away our
youth. It always comes to us with a great
shock when some younger person suddenly
reveals to us the first knowledge that we no
longer are in the company of the young ;
that we have joined the great army of the
old.

" I cannot sit while an old lady stands,"
said a sweet young girl one day to a woman
who had not even begun to think of herself

as more than middle-aged, and it really gave her quite a turn. In our attentions to those who are older than ourselves it is well to employ a little tact, not emphasizing too greatly the difference between them and ourselves.

I read some time ago a very interesting story of an old mother in New England, whose children were solicitous to save her every possible trouble. They never let her do a single thing. She was shielded from every rough wind. If she attempted to walk across the room, John or Mary was at hand, exclaiming, "What do you want, mother? Let me do that for you."

She was in fact surrounded with attentions every minute of her life, yet somehow the old lady was unhappy and dissatisfied, and grew harder to please every day. One day there came a telegram to the house. Some member of the family at a distance had suddenly been taken ill, and it was imperative that John and Mary should at once take the first train and haste to the assistance of the invalid. There was no time even to send to the next house for a neighbor to come in. Mother had to be left alone, and great was the grief about it. All in a rush and a flurry the young people got their things on and whirled away to the station.

The moment they were fairly out of sight and the railroad whistle had shown that the train was off, mother, notwithstanding her threescore years and ten, jumped from her chair and executed a little jig of delight. Then she went upstairs, got all the soiled clothes in the house, came down, built a fire, put on the wash-boiler, and did with the greatest glee an old-fashioned washing.

When I read this, I remembered an old lady who had scandalized the neighbors by doing a similar thing in the absence of her niece with whom she lived. They saw a row of blankets on the line, and to their horror observed that the oldest lady in the house was superintending this unwonted laundry work. Bless her heart ! she was happy, even if it was too much for her.

Let us be very considerate and very amiable and lovely in our whole demeanor toward those who are older than ourselves. Only thus shall we be really what we should be, and shall earn a right to expect in our turn consideration when we too grow old.

" If mother would listen to me, dears,
   She would freshen that faded gown ;
She would sometimes take an hour's rest,
   And sometimes a trip to town.
And it shouldn't be all for the children,
   The fun, and the cheer, and the play ;
With the patient droop on the tired mouth,
   And the ' Mother has had her day ! '

" True, mother has had her day, dears,
   When you were her babies three,
And she stepped about the farm and the house,
   As busy as ever a bee ;

15

When she rocked you all to sleep, dears,
    And sent you all to school,
And wore herself out, and did without,
    And lived by the Golden Rule.

" And so your turn has come, dears;
    Her hair is growing white;
And her eyes are gaining the far-away look
    That peers beyond the night.
One of these days in the morning,
    Mother will not be here;
She will fade away into silence;
    The mother so true and dear.

" Then, what will you do in the daylight,
    And what in the gloaming dim;
And father, tired and lonesome then,
    Pray, what will you do for him?
If you want to keep your mother,
    You must make her rest to-day;
Must give her a share in the frolic,
    And draw her into the play.

" And, if your mother would listen to me, dears
    She'd buy her a gown of silk,
With buttons of royal velvet,
    And ruffles as white as milk;
And she'd let you do the trotting,
    While she sat still in her chair
That mother should have it hard all through,
    It strikes me. isn't fair.

## A TALK ABOUT CLOTHES.

You fancied, my dear Mr. Gradgrind, that you were doing a very fine and independent thing when you humiliated your daughter by appearing at her college on commencement day in rough homespun clothing, with unbrushed hat, unpolished boots, and a general air of coarseness and disarrangment about your dress; this, too, when it was well known that you were a man of large wealth, and that it was a mere eccentricity which made you, and always makes you, different from the people among whom you move, because you pride yourself on dressing just as you like.

Far from doing a praiseworthy thing, you were trampling upon one of our most important statutes in the social code. A thoroughly agreeable man or woman is always dressed appropriately for the function in which he or she shares, or for the business in hand. It would be quite absurd for you or me to wear evening-dress in the kitchen or in the furrow. An organdie gown, with trimmings of lace and chiffon, does not harmonize with the wash-tub; nor, if the work in hand happens to be baking the week's bread do we invest ourselves with our most beautiful tailor-made gown, or our new and elegant silk and velvet dress.

There is a fitness which should be consulted in all matters of clothing, and it is no virtue to despise one's raiment. Every one should dress as well as he can afford to. Shakespeare's dictum about clothing, to "have it as costly as thy purse can buy," is a very good one for us all, especially as things which are good to begin with outlast, by several times their price, the cheap imitation, which is ruined by a shower or faded by the sun, and which loses all semblance of elegance after a very short season's wearing.

To impoverish ourselves, however, for finery, to wear things for which we cannot pay, to be in debt to our tailor and our dressmaker, is decidedly foolish and wicked. Always observing the proper degree of honesty and common-sense, however, we should dress as well as we can, and we owe it to our friends and to our neighbors to present a pleasing appearance to them when they meet us at home or abroad.

Especially is it a good plan for every one to come to the table neatly and becomingly dressed. We should not come to our own dinner-table without making some effort to look fresh, neat, and tidy. Concerning this grace of tidiness, an interesting writer has said,—

"In days gone by, before the new woman appeared upon the scene of action, girls were rigidly taught the good old-fashioned principle of tidiness. 'Neatness' hardly expresses my meaning as well as does the quaint, old-time word. To be 'tidy,' Webster tells us, is to be 'arranged in good order; neat; kept in proper and becoming neatness.' Nowadays girls are neat to a certain extent and in a certain way. They bathe freely and wear clean clothes; but are they tidy? Frequently, they are not. Their hair is often loose and prone to tumble down, their gloves are sometimes ripped at the finger-tips, and one or two buttons are lacking from their boots. The stock-collar is often fastened on with an ordinary white pin that is very obvious, and the veil has occasionally a hole over the nose or chin. Our girl is charming; but is she as careful as she should be?

"The other day I was making a morning call at a friend's house, and there met another caller, a woman who made a most agreeable impression upon me. She was not elaborately dressed, but her black tailor-made gown fitted her well, and there was not a spot nor a speck of dust on it. I knew that it had been brushed carefully before she left her room. Her linen collar and cuffs were snowy white, and did not twist or shift from their proper places. Her gloves did not wrinkle, and buttoned smoothly over the wrists; her shoes were like the rest of her attire—dainty; and her bonnet rested firmly and straight on soft brown hair that, while wavy and fluffy, was neatly dressed, and so securely pinned that I fancy a high wind would not have caused it to come down. A thin veil covered a fresh complexion and bright face. The *tout ensemble* gave one the idea of daintiness and delicate finish. In speaking of this woman afterwards to a man who knows her, I said :

"'There is something about her appearance that charms one. What is the secret?'

"'I will tell you,' he said. 'She is a well-groomed woman. There are never any rough or loose ends about her.'

"'You mean that she is tidy,' I said to him.

"'You call it "tidy," I say "well-groomed." We both mean the same thing.'

"However one may express it—in sporting terms or with the old-fashioned word—is the condition not well worth striving for? Nothing is so destructive to illusion, so detrimental to the fascination of beauty or personal charm, as the lack of this quality."

It certainly adds very much to the pleasure of an occasion and to the delight of everyday life to mingle with people whose outward appearance is attractive. There is, in fact, a certain toning up of good manners with the putting on of our best clothes. I once heard a lady say, when asked why she

wore a certain bright bow in the schoolroom,
her work being to teach a number of restless
little boys : "I find that my days go better
when I am prettily dressed. The boys like
to see the bright color and they behave
much better than they would if I came care-
lessly dressed."

"Mamma," said a dear child, surveying
sadly his mother's mourning robes, "I wish
you wore pretty gowns as Harry's mother
does." The mother was wise and unselfish
enough to heed the child. She took off her
sombre, clinging garments, dressed herself
in white with bright ribbons, and never
again wore the depressing dress which her
child did not like.

She felt that her duty to the living was as
great as the respect she owed to the dead,
and she knew that if the child's father could
speak from the silence to which he had gone,
he would rather see her do that which was
for the child's good than offer up a sacrifice
to his memory.

"My little boy," said a lady to me, "is so
very fond of having on his best clothes, and
I notice that when he goes out with me
dressed in his nicest suit he holds up his
head and behaves in a most attentive and
deferential manner. It seems as if the
putting on of his best things involves in him
a decided improvement of behavior."

We all know just what it means. With
assumption of raiment for an occasion

comes unconsciously the feeling of ceremony and the desire to live up to our clothes.
In a sense we all live up to our clothes.
Every woman knows that when she puts
on a beautiful, fresh, unsoiled pair of gloves
she cannot afford to have the rest of her
toilette conspicuously below the standard
which the gloves have set.

Still, we must not depend for making an
agreeable impression exclusively upon our
dress. I once had a neighbor—she has long
since passed away, so that I may speak of
her without danger of wounding any one's
feelings—who thought that dress was the
beginning and end of everything. She
had neither wit, good manners, nor much
intelligence ; but she spent quantities of
money on her personal adornment. Her
diamonds represented a fortune, and she
was so fond of them that she frequently
loaded her fingers with rings outside of her
gloves—of course the most ill-bred thing
any one could possibly do.

When I used to hear ungrammatical expressions, double negatives, and slang falling from her lips, and contrasted her style of
talk with her latest fashions brought from
Paris and Vienna, I used to think nothing
could be so vulgar and coarse as an ignorant woman bedecked in finery and jewels,
the very beauty of her dress calling attention
to her innate defects.

All one really needs is a simple, well-fitted

gown, appropriate to the place and the hour where it is worn. When we put our clothes on we should be able to forget them, and the best-dressed woman is always the one whose dress does not call attention to itself. Mrs. John Hancock is said to have remarked that she could never admire a girl who thought about her clothes, or, on the other hand, whose clothes were neglected.

After all, a sweet and gracious manner and a presence of dignity are of all things most important. Of a very popular woman it was once said : "She never wore ornaments, but she was always well-dressed. A simple, well-fitted gown, and hair tastefully disposed, were all one could see of any effort to make her person pleasing, and these seemed to be forgotten, and, I believe, were forgotten, the moment she entered society. When friends were around her she had no thought but of them—no desire but to give and receive pleasure. If she was asked to sing, she sang, and, if it ministered to the pleasure of others, she sang patiently, even to weariness. She was as intelligent and stimulating in sober conversation as she was playful in spirit, and though she loved general society, and mingled freely in it, not a breath of slander ever sullied her name, and not an emotion was ever excited by her that did not do her honor. Every man admired and honored her, and every woman — a much greater marvel—spoke in her praise.

Many a belle, dressed at the height of fashion, entered her presence only to become insignificant. Diamonds were forgotten and splendid dress was unmentioned, while her sweet presence, her self-forgetful devotion to the pleasure of others, and her gentle manners were recalled and dwelt upon with unalloyed delight."

It is quite legitimate to say a great deal about dress in a book on the art of being agreeable. Cuffs and collars, for instance, should be immaculate ; everything about us should be trim and pleasing. Mr. Ruskin, writing for young girls, epitomizes the matter so far as they are concerned :

"Dress as plainly as your parents will allow you, but in bright colors, if they become you, and in the best materials ; that is to say, in those which will wear longest. When you are really in want of a new dress, buy it or make it in the fashion, but never quit an old one merely because it has become unfashionable. And if the fashion be costly, you need not follow it. You may wear broad stripes or narrow, bright colors or dark, short petticoats or long (in moderation) as the public wish you ; but you must not buy yards of useless stuff to make a knot or a flounce of; nor drag them behind you over the ground. And your walking dress must never touch the ground at all. I have lost much of the faith I once had in the common-sense and even in the personal

delicacy of the present race of average Eng-
lishwomen, by seeing how they will allow
their dresses to sweep the streets, if it is the
fashion to be scavengers. If you can afford
it, get your dresses made by a good dressmaker, with utmost attainable precision
and perfection. And be sure of this, that
although in a truly Christian land every
young girl would be dressed beautifully and
delightfully,—in this entirely heathen and
Baal-worshipping land of ours not one girl
in ten has either decent or healthy clothing;
and that you have no business, till this be
amended, to wear anything fine yourself,
but *are bound to use your full strength and
resources* to dress as many of your poor
neighbors as you can. What of fine dress
your people insist upon your wearing, take
—and wear proudly and prettily for their
sakes; but so far as in you lies, be sure
that every day you are laboring to clothe
some poorer creatures. Devote a part of
every day to thorough needlework, in making as pretty dresses as you can for poor people, who have not time nor taste to make
them nicely for themselves. You are to
show them in your own wearing what is
modestly right and graceful; and to help
them to choose what will be prettiest and
most becoming in their own station. If they
see that you never try to dress above yours,
they will not try to dress above theirs."

## OUT OF THE PROCESSION.

A man who has all his life been accustomed to activity, whose duties have been insistent and pressing, whose opinion has been sought and advice accepted by many, finds it a terribly wearing experience to be laid aside. Age comes, or creeping paralysis, or ill health in some form, or an accident saps the man's strength in his prime, and the procession goes on, but he is no longer in the ranks. Perhaps the day dawns when he is forced to say to himself, if indeed he does not say it to his friends, " I am no longer essential to any one. Nobody needs me. My kindred could do as well without me as with me. No work requires my hand. My services are important no longer. I have fallen out, and the rest of the day is a waiting for the end."

A man may say and feel this with entire truth, and the busy world may indeed seem to need him no longer. If his temperament, notwithstanding his infirmities, still inclines him to action, if he have not a competence and is aware that his continued life means harder work for those he loves, so that he is forced to consider himself an encumbrance, a dead weight on their hands, then he is obliged to eat bitter bread, and resignation is hard to find.

In such circumstances, his very unhappiness, his sense of being *de trop*, and his enforced helplessness in a distasteful environment may combine to render him morose, sullen, and disagreeable. The one thing left to him, the one possible attainment which yet may be his, seems the utterly impracticable and not-to-be-dreamed-of result, when he thinks of it : how shall he, no longer in the procession, wear a smiling face, speak cheerily, play with the grandchildren, sit overlooked in the corner, and preserve serenity, put down querulous complaint, and set the slow pace of his waning days to the sunshine of an accepted providential dispensation !

It *is* hard, dear friend, and it's going to be hard all the while. But you may make it easier if you choose. " The cup which My Father hath given Me, shall I not drink it ? " " Even so, Father, for so it seemeth good in Thy sight." What our Lord said in His supreme hour is the test of obedience and acquiescence for His disciples, in their lesser hours of extremity.

Accept the situation. You are out of the procession. Well, then, become a philosophical onlooker. You have earned by long service a right to sit in the balcony and wave a flag as the marching legions pass.

The old thrill will come to you now and then.  You can even shout when the boys you have trained go by, laurelled and victorious.  Having borne the burden and heat of the day, bear to wait awhile for the Master's "Well done."  Be resigned, and be acquiescent, because this is God's appointment for you; then people will no longer say, "What a fretful old gentleman General —— has become!" but, "If ever there was a hero on earth, it is General ——.  So brave, so cheery, so agreeable, though he is laid aside.  Well, if ever a man earned the right to rest, he did."

## THE GOOD LISTENER.

This chapter is meant for everybody ; you cannot afford to skip it, for it is written for you.

One of the most delightful people we ever meet is not famous for fluent conversation so much as for attentive listening. I was a very small child when my father one day said to me : "Always look at a person who is speaking to you and listen with all your might." This little rule of looking steadily at a friend and wearing an air of interest while talking with him is of great importance, commonplace as it seems. To carry on a conversation with an absent-minded acquaintance who stares out of the window or perhaps turns over the pages of a book, while you are talking, apparently indifferent to the subject in hand, is one of life's minor trials. In one of Anthony Trollope's stories of English life there is depicted a most charming woman. She is the idol of everybody, popular and successful in society beyond all the women of her time. On investigation, the secret of her charm is found to be that she is always a most agreeable listener, flattering the men about her, and the women too, by her well-bred and pleased attention to all that they say. The good listener does not interrupt the conversation, even if his friend is a little diffuse and his meaning involved. He lets him go on, never showing by word or gesture that he is tired, never supplying a word, but patiently waiting until the other has finished his sentence. The temptation to supply a word for which your friend is mentally searching is sometimes great, but, as a rule, to do this is injudicious and impolite. It is an implication that the friend cannot find the word for himself. One should be more than careful when the friend has an impediment in his speech. The tongue of the stammerer does not wish assistance, although it sometimes appears as if this would be welcome, and for our comfort we may assume that he is less disturbed by his infirmity than we are.

To listen agreeably one must feel an interest in what is being said. Sometimes this is very difficult. The subject may be foreign to you, and again there are people who talk in a sort of monotone, with few cadences and very little variety in their manner of speech. I know several women whose conversation has upon me a most lulling effect, and if I am tired or a little inclined to sleep, it is with a great effort that I keep myself from nodding while the flow of their monotonous talk goes on like Tennyson's brook. Still, one must say to one-self, "*Noblesse oblige,*" and no matter how little you may know of your friend's subject or how wearisome the talk may be, it is still the better part to act as if you were interested, and in this way, before you are aware of it, an interest will probably be created.

The truly unselfish person is interested in others, whether or not they are in themselves attractive, but such altruism is a matter not only of Christian charity but of social training.

One of the things which ought to be taught in the schools is the practice of listening to what is going on.

One needs only to watch the different faces in an audience to learn how few people comparatively have learned the art of listening as it should be acquired. Do not suppose that the minister or orator or platform speaker is not affected by the inattention of the individuals in the audience. Sometimes when one is in the full tide of an eloquent address, he will find himself quite thrown off the track by seeing some one in front of him pull out and carefully consult his watch, as much as to say: "Will this wearisome person never get done?" A look of bored indifference or aversion is a check to one who is endeavoring to appeal to a throng; and if this is so, how much more must it be the case when the question is one of a talk in the parlor or of a *tête-à-tête.*

16

"What is the secret of Miss Blank's popularity ? " I once asked, mentioning a spinster well on towards fifty, of no particular attractiveness, neither endowed abundantly with good looks or cleverness, but absolutely one of the most welcome comers in all social gatherings that I have ever seen. The answer was, "She always listens as if you were the only person in the world, and as if she cared very much for what you were telling her."

Here is a talent which any one of us may cultivate. Some of us will always be tongue-tied, and some of us can never hope to be brilliant or accomplished or to make a great figure in the world ; we have our limitations ; but we may listen with perfect amiability and attention to people who talk to us, and if we do this, we shall never lack a welcome. There is, you see, a very graceful deference displayed in the mere formality of paying attention. It is as if one should say : "It was worth while for me to have met you, and what you are telling me is of consequence and I shall be happier for having heard it." To oil the machinery of home life and make it run smoothly and without friction, no one is more successful than the ordinary listener who listens well.

Another point to be remembered, and one which the listener would do well to cultivate, is to identify the people one casually meets. It is said that the Prince of Wales has a wonderful gift of recollecting the names and faces of people whom he meets, so that if an obscure country clergyman comes up to London and is presented to the prince, meeting him of course only in a transient way, a year after the prince will recollect and address him by name. It always delights us to find that at least we have made a sufficient impression to have our personality recalled. Many of us find it exceedingly difficult and almost impossible to match names and faces. We can remember a face but not a name, or a name but not a face, and we resort sometimes to all sorts of expedients to hide our infirmity from those we meet. Thus I once said to a young woman who rushed up most cordially to meet me on the street as if she were overjoyed at the encounter: "Where are you living now?" The answer was most confusing. It was: "Just where I did when you called on me,"—which gave me no clue whatever to her identity. Frankness in this instance would have been wiser to begin with, and as confession seemed likely to wound her feelings, I had to let my friend go without being at all sure which one of a number of interesting young people of my slighter acquaintance she was. It would be well for us if faces and names do not readily impress themselves upon our subconsciousness to make a mental effort to gain strength in this direction. One of the most dearly

loved clergymen whom I know remembers
the children in a very large Sunday school
by their Christian names, and whenever they
meet him, he wins their affection by a
genuine interest in their home affairs. A
talent of this sort is not given to us all, but it
is well worth a great effort to obtain, and,
like most gifts, we may have it if we choose
to pay the price in eager and earnest attention and in caring for those whom we
meet. Indeed, let us cultivate sedulously a
talent for loving our kind, so that people,
wherever we touch their lives, shall give us
of their best, so that we may never meet
any one, however humble, however exalted,
who will not receive from us, in some
measure, a benediction. This it is to be
genuinely unselfish, to have the love that
seeketh not her own, and vaunteth not
herself, but constantly imitates Him who
came to minister to the world.

## TEACHERS AND SCHOLARS.

So large a portion of our lives is spent in the schoolroom that it is quite worth our while to consider the question of good manners there.

" I wish that the teacher had lessons to learn,"
Said Molly, the wise little elf,
" She would never make them so hard and so long,
If she had but to do them herself."

And the teacher, at home in the twilight that eve,
Sighed, " If the dear children but knew,
How easy it is, and how glad are the days
When we have only lessons to do."

Much depends on the teacher's power to clothe a subject with interest, and to stimulate in his pupils the desire to discover things for themselves ; there is no royal road to excellence, and we all alike, modern methods notwithstanding, have to creep before we walk, and drudge before we acquire and accumulate.

Parents owe it to their children to establish pleasant social intercourse between the home and the school. Invite the teacher home to tea, or to dinner make a little party for the teacher now and then, when Harry or Molly has done particularly well. Let the teacher know how pleased you are at your child's progress.

While not entertaining too readily a child's complaints, still it is a parent's bounden duty to investigate when there are complaints, and find out whether there is occasion for them. A sensitive or diffident child should not be at the mercy of a severe or partial teacher, who has favorites and shows that she prefers one of her pupils to another. Balances must be kept even.

New methods in teaching have supplanted the somewhat primitive ways once in vogue, but it is still true that if Nature have not endowed a child with capacity, money will not buy that necessary adjunct to education. Many mistakes are made in the schoolroom, and parents are often mistaken in their estimate of the intellectual powers of their offspring, yet, to the end of time, there will be children clever in some directions and dull in others, languid and indolent children who need the spur of emulation, and bright, ambitious children, who must be held in check lest they learn too rapidly. An excellent feature of the educational practice of our period is that even when, as in our public schools, children must be taught in masses, there is a strong effort on the part of teachers to study the individual child, while in private schools, small classes

and much attention to the individual has
become the rule.

Out in the great world there is the roar
and clash and shock of battle, and the tu-
mult is incessant.   On 'Change there is always agitation.   But wars and rumors of
wars do not trouble the schoolroom, and the
desks are filled with papers and pencils,
sunny heads bend over books, and fingers
draw maps and cast up accounts.   The next
generation is in the schoolroom.   A few
flying years and it will be in the thick of the
strife, as we are now ; but to-day it is in training, and its trials and triumphs are under
the eye of the pedagogue.

It is a period of fierce struggle and rivalry,
a time of stubborn competition, and many
must sooner or later be numbered among
the unsuccessful,—many, too, who to-day
seem well fitted for success.   In the ranks
of the liberally educated, of those who have
been graduated from our colleges, there will
be a certain percentage who will find that
admirable vantage-ground where there is
said to be always room ; they will aim for,
and arrive at the top.   Others will do very
respectable work, but will never make a
special mark, will not be heard of beyond
their own towns, and will not be eminent
even in a narrow and restricted sphere ; and
still others will wear on from youth to middle age, distinctly and sorrowfully unsuccessful.

A peculiarity of some unsuccessful men is that they do not seem to lack perseverance. They try and try, knocking at every door, pulling every string, and wearying their friends with the sight of their vain endeavors. One such used to pass me daily on the street, a man of refined appearance, scholarly aspect and gentle breeding. His life, as I learned later, was one of heroic endurance ; in the care of a relative bound for years to a couch of agonizing pain he showed the most tender and tireless devotion, performing menial services with his own hands, and never allowing a hint of the privations which he bore without complaint to cloud her uncertain sunshine. But she died and he soon followed, the neighbors said as a result of poverty and discouragement and debt, a lawyer without a client, an able man, for whom there never seemed an opening or even a foothold in the line of advancement.

Another such struggling man I knew intimately, and can testify that neither weakness of will, nor vice of any sort, nor indolence, nor anything, except, perhaps, an excessive caution, kept him always at the rear. Others, who started with him, achieved success—some signally, some moderately. But he went from youth to gray hairs, ever poorer, ever less able to cope with life, ever more and more unsuccessful till the curtain dropped.

To be successful one must needs be
somewhat aggressive. Not unamiable, but
amiability must be buttressed round and
bolstered up by a great strength of will and
a resolute determination not to yield an
inch of ground once honestly gained. The
aggressive man conquers his way inch by
inch, and he loses no advantage once acquired. There must be, too, the ability to
hold fast to a position, and to strike roots
deep in one place. The person who likes
frequent change, who is over-sensitive and
easily rebuffed, who allows circumstances
to interfere with him, instead of ruling over
circumstances, is pre-doomed to be unsuccessful.

There is also the question of sensible and
judicious choice in the outset, and here
parents come into the case. Men are pushed
into business when nature meant them for
professions, for art, for teaching, for the
pulpit. Men have been unwisely urged to
choose the pulpit when, beyond piety, they
had no vocation for that particular field of
service, when they would have been at
home behind the counter or behind the plow
rather than at the sacred desk. Too late the
mistake was discovered and very likely
deplored, but the man externally had become of his profession and could not adopt
another, but had to go on in a course
shadowed by blighted hopes to the very
end. In selecting the life career it behooves

every one of us to be conscientious, to be careful in taking account of predilection, of talent and of probable opportunity. A boy should be wisely advised ; sometimes urged to wait before deciding on what is to influence all his earthly years ; sometimes, for his own good, overruled.

The foundations for success or failure are being laid during the years of pupilage. Some children need very careful manual training ; others are deft-handed and graceful, understand tools readily, and have constructive ability,—these are in want of intellectual discipline, must have mind and heart cultivated. Make the school life *tell*, and to do so, see that the child loves the schoolroom and that every day is a step in the process of natural and proper development.

Do not suffer the children to be self-conscious. In our well-meant efforts to keep children from vanity, we frequently foster a quality as unfortunate. A mother says, quoting from her book of experience :

"I know at least three ladies, each distinguished for mental and moral strength, who will in their weaker moments feel themselves awkward, ugly, uncouth, to the day of their death because of childish impressions. Mrs. R., one of the brightest women I have ever met, said to me : 'When I was a child I was always being told how big I was, how difficult it was to make me "look anyhow" in my clothes. My sister, who was slim and natty, was spoken of over and over in my hearing as a child who could be "made something of." I was called raw-boned and gawky till I believed myself to be a blot upon creation.'

" 'To this day,' says my brilliant friend H., 'I am self-conscious upon entering a room, feeling that every one must be criticising me. My grandmother, or rather step-grandmother, who brought me up from a baby, never let me forget that my shoulders were "square," my gait "ungainly," that I was a "black little thing not fit to be seen." The impressions burned into my baby consciousness can never be erased while I am clothed in this mortal body.'

"The third example was so pretty as a child that her mother felt it a duty to kill the upcomings of vanity. The girl, whose love of approbation was great, was made by this treatment to think constantly of herself. Many times a day she ran to the glass to see if she were really such 'a dowdy little thing.' She examined her fair, round arms; were they really fat and coarse—'Palmer arms?' as her mother said. Grandmother Palmer was short and plump and red-faced. The granddaughter was a very rosebud in freshness and purity of tint. Yet the girl was tortured by self-consciousness, and so hungry was she for admiration, approval rather, so starved was she for mother-brooding and mother-cuddling that anybody who praised her, or flattered her, or was pleasant to her, found easy access to her heart."

Suppose this mother had said : " You are like a flower for freshness and attractiveness. God has made you so. Think how you can make others happy by this gift of beauty. Be like a wild rose in the hedge that is unconscious of itself, but is the joy of every one who sees it." The "pretty girl," taught thus the value of beauty and its natural relation to a true and noble life, thinks no longer of her looks, and falls into her place of world-brighteners and joy-makers as naturally as a flower blooms in the garden or by the wayside.

The girl who has no form, the awkward girl, should have her thoughts drawn away from physical defects, which are generally immaturities ; she may be judiciously praised for success in her studies, for helpfulness at home, for any strong point that she may possess. She may be taught to feel that she is "mother's right hand," and have a healthful pride awakened in qualities that have nothing to do with her physique. Secure in the love and approbation and admiration of her home friends, the daughter feels only natural, proper care for what others may think of her. The awkward girl, knowing that she is prized at home, becomes unconsciously graceful through happiness and self-respect.

The nest is for brooding, the home is for

loving, teaching, training. Most unfortunate is the child whose heart is starved at home. Seeking food among strangers, she may receive poison instead. The girl in whose heart nestles the thought, " Mother thinks I am pretty," has no further care about the matter. The girl whose father is also " admirer" will not surrender her heart for a few tender phrases.

This view of the case, that we must be liberal with praise and very sparing of blame, is as needful to the teacher who honestly strives to advance her pupils, or his, as for the parent. A great many hours of a great many days are passed under the eye of the teacher. Why should they not be the happiest hours of juvenile life?

## REST WHEN YOU ARE TIRED.

Middle-aged women ought not to have anxious faces. Lines there may be of care, of sorrow, of struggle, but we women growing older have a right to serenity, and on our brows the angel of household joy and tenderness should evermore press the seal of peace. The inner light, shining from the soul to the eyes, should be divinely beautiful.

But, dear ladies, to have this sweetness of expression, you must rest when you are tired. It has been observed wisely that :

Form develops first from rest and the strength that comes of rest. A tired, weakly figure will sag and bend and want elasticity. Overworked figures settle down and lose two inches of height by the pressing together of the parts of the body. That is why women seem and are shorter after middle age. On rest depends the length and suppleness of limb, and women should know how to take advantage, to secure rest and conserve strength. Girls must be trained to take rest at proper seasons, whether they feel tired or not, and the woman must continue this exact and special care of herself as the foundation of her well-being.  A day or two laying off at the right time, having her breakfast in bed and spending the day in the luxury of a wrapper and a lounge, will make the difference between a blithe, active creature the next few weeks, or one who goes about with a constant ache and fatigue.

Dr. Hosmer, the father of Harriet Hosmer, the sculptor, one of the acutest of New England physicians, used to drive around the circle of his practice in house-cleaning seasons telling women to lie down and rest when tired, as half an hour at full length on a lounge would refresh the whole body more than three hours sitting in a chair.  The periodical rest should be insisted on by every mother as long as she lives to watch over her daughter.  Without it shoulders grow bowed and the gait dragging.  With rest the step is elastic, the form well upheld, the bust firm, the limbs retain elegance and shape.  Work while you work, and rest while you rest, should be the rule for every girl and woman.

After advising the duty of rest, it will sound strange to urge the value of hard work in keeping a good form, but the two supplement each other.  Hard work is not overwork, but rapid, steady work that pulls muscle into play and sends the blood and sweat flowing finely.  Perhaps you will bear better what that polished physician and man of the world, Dr. Weir Mitchell, says on the subject : "I think it fortunate when women are so situated as to have to do things about the household which exact vigorous use of the upper extremities. Nothing is a better ally against nervousness or irritabilility in any one than outdoor exercise or pretty violent use of the muscles."

Speaking of woman's work, that keen-sighted and sharp-tongued critic, the late lamented Gail Hamilton, said :

"I do not say that a man's work may not be harder for an hour, or five or ten hours, more exhaustive of mental and vital power, more exclusive of all diversions than his wife's for the same time. It may or may not be ; quite as often the latter as the former ; but I do say that severe pre-arranged, intermittent labor wears less upon the temper, the nerves, and the spirits,—that is, upon body and soul,—than lighter, confused, unintermitting labor. Work that enlists the energies and the enthusiasm will weary, but the weariness itself is welcome, and brings with it a satisfaction,—the pleasant sense of something accomplished. The multiplicity of a woman's labors distracts as well as wearies, and each one is so petty that she has scarcely anything to look back on. Not one of them is great enough to brace and stimulate, and altogether they form a multitudinous heap, and not a mountain. It is a round of endless detail : little,

insignificant, provoking items that she gets
no credit for doing, but fatal discredit for
leaving undone. Nobody notices that things
are as they should be ; but if things are not as
they should be, it were better for her that a
millstone were hanged about her neck, etc. ! "

Even the children, darlings as they are,
do not invariably bring mothers an un-
mixed delight. All their weariness and
fretfulness and tumbles and aches are
poured into her lap. She has no division of
labor, no concentration of forces ; no five
or ten hours devoted to housework, and two
or three to her children, taking them into
her heart to do good like a medicine. They
patter through every hour, to stay her from
doing with her might any of the many
things which her hands find to do. Nothing keeps limits ; everything laps over.
God has given her a love so inexhaustible
that, notwithstanding the washings and
watchings, the sewing and dressing which
children necessitate, notwithstanding the
care, check, the pull-back, the weariness,
the heartsickness, which they occasion, the
"little hindering things" are—my pen is
not wont to be timid, but it shrinks from
attempting to say what little ones are to a
mother. But divine arrangement does not
prevent human drawback ; and looking not
at inward solace, but outward business, it remains true that the business of providing for
the wants of a family is not of that smooth,

17

uncreaking nature to the mother that it is to
the father.　Let a man take two or three little
children—two or three ?　Let him take one !
—of one, two, three, or four years of age,
to his shop, or stall, or office, and take care
of him all the time for a week, and he will
see what I mean.

To every mother, even the most fond and
devoted, there comes a moment when the
very best thing she can do for herself and
her children is to let somebody else take
care of them for awhile.　I have often
thought that, among our endless societies
and associations, there might to advantage
be included another composed of unmarried
ladies, sweet, cheery, faded spinsters, and
lovely young girls, whose function should
be to relieve wearied-out mothers, now for
a forenoon, again for a day, and yet again
for a week or a fortnight.　This Society for
the Succor of Self-denying Mothers would
need little organization.　It should have
a membership of sunny-hearted women,
who would not mind staying at home
from church sometimes, so that while they
amused restless little boys and girls, or
crooned to fretful babies, the mothers might
have the almost forgotten delight of sitting
comfortably in the family pew.　The work
to be done would need no flourish of
trumpets, would not figure in the newspapers, but the recording pen of the angel
on high would write it down.

Miss Anna C. Brackett, who is an authority on the subject of gaining freedom and power by judicious repose, enjoins on women in her admirable book, "The Technique of Rest," to learn to keep still outwardly, even as to hands and the tips of your fingers, as to feet and head, and you will find rest and quiet coming to the mind as a result. If you are ill, lie quiet if it be possible, and it will generally be found so. Lie still, and don't allow yourself to toss about. Sit still when you sit, and stand still when you must stand. Try this constantly and persistently and you will not fail of help. Allow yourself to make no motion that has not a purpose and an aim ; if you find yourself moving unnecessarily, call yourself back to quietness. No one can tell how much of the beautiful serenity of the Quakers comes from the outward stillness and quiet of their worship. Watch other people to be convinced how much muscular and nervous force is actually thrown away for nothing. Do not allow yourself to move nervously fast, and the more nervous you are, the more deliberate all motions should be. Force yourself to move slowly even if you are in a hurry. In walking, the tread of the city policeman is an excellent model for one to imitate, though there is no danger that you will succeed in copying it exactly. When at your desk, and with not much time to spare,

the pencil falls on the floor, and the ruler
won't be picked up, your eyeglass string
catches on a button, you can't find the
blotter, and the paper on which were the
memoranda you were copying just gets up
from the desk and plunges, without any
obvious motive-power but its own will, into
the waste-basket; or when, another day,
scissors slip to the floor, the knot which
you are sure you had made at the end of
your basting-thread is not there, do not
lose precious time, and sacrifice poise and
equilibrium to fretting and folly.

"If," adds this judicious mentor, "you
must have tonics, take those also from
Him, in sunshine, pure air, exercise, regular hours, healthful food, and, above all
perhaps, in sleep.  Religiously avoid all
others.  It is vain hoping to restore nerve-
power by recourse to medicine.  All such
attempts are but patches, which only take
from the garment, making the rent worse.
An English physician has recently said of
the maladies which imply or consist in loss
of nerve-power, such as suppressed gout,
hysteria, neuralgia, insomnia, chorea, epi-
lepsy, melancholia, and general loss of
mental control, that 'all this class of ills
are, as a rule, whether they be hereditary
in their origin or not—and very often they
are hereditary—extremely gradual and slow
in their onset, arising, as they do, from
deep-rooted, constitutional causes.'  He

maintains, therefore, that they can be successfully combated 'only by very cautious and gradual remedies—remedies which do not cause any reaction, but which slowly steal into the system, and restore its strength by gradually accumulating, without stimulating, the resources from which nerve-power is derived. Strong nerve-tonics are in such cases mischievous, and sedatives positively injurious. A healthy plan of life, with air, exercise, and nutritive food are of the first importance.' This point can hardly be enough insisted upon. What you have done by a long series of drafts upon your nerve strength, whether necessary or not, can be made up only by a long series of efforts at patience and of will-power to keep yourself still and in the way of recovery."

After all, and almost to be regarded as the conclusion of the whole matter, there is no pillow for the weary head, no cordial for the faint, like the realized sense of the Divine, ever-present goodness.

There is no rest for the weary heart, no balm for the sorrows of life, no ease for the back bowed with the daily burden like the realized thought of the everlasting love. Blessed thought which comes to us in the night-watches calming disturbance, and soothing the eyes which care holds from slumber. Sweet words of faith and dependence spoken by holy men of old sing

themselves to the tune of our modern
melodies, as our lips move softly and we
say, "The Lord is nigh unto all them that
call upon him, to all that call upon him in
truth. Hear my prayer, O Lord, give ear
to my supplications. I stretch forth my
hands unto thee; my soul thirsteth after
thee, as a thirsty land. Lord, thou hast
been our dwelling-place in all generations."
Verse after verse from the Psalms rises in
memory, as stars arise in the sky, and,
though we may be grieving over our dead,
or, yet sadder experience, grieving over our
living dear ones, we still can say, "Because thy loving-kindness is better than life,
my lips shall praise thee. Thus will I bless
thee while I live, I will lift up my hands in
thy name. Because thou hast been my
help, therefore in the shadow of thy wings
will I rejoice."

In the midst of the day's toil, as in the
wakefulness of the night, it is blessed to
call to mind the assurances given by our
heavenly Father that He will always support and sustain us. "As thy day, shall
thy strength be." "Fear not, little flock.
It is your Father's good pleasure to give
you the kingdom." "Behold, the Lord's
hand is not shortened, that it cannot save,
neither is his ear heavy, that it cannot
hear."

The disciple of Christ need never be cast
down nor discouraged, let circumstances

be adverse or opportune. For the one cable
which holds against all strain of our infirmities, our wants, or our yielding to temptation is the cable of the ceaseless love of
God. We are kept by the power of God
through faith unto salvation. We do not
keep ourselves. We are kept.

When we look about us in the world we
cannot help seeing that earthly love and
human friendship are subject to changing
conditions. The staunchest plank of human
affection may give way in a storm. The
wife may grow cold and indifferent to the
husband of her youth ; the husband may
cease to show the tenderness and consideration which once made her life a dream of
delight. The child going forth from the
home and forming other relationships, apparently is weaned from the early loyalty
and the fondness he once felt for the parents
to whom he was all in all. The father and
mother may be disappointed in the daughter and the son, and no longer treat them
with the proud fondness of a happier time.
Brothers and sisters drift apart, and perhaps
for weeks and months together they do not
mention the names which once were spoken
every day. Mrs. Hemans made a true state-
ment of fact in her poem, "The Graves of a
Household," about the scattering of many a
family who "grew in beauty side by side,
and filled one home with glee," but we do
not always wait for the cold hand of death

to come and separate beloved kindred.
Life wields a surer and sharper knife of division than death.   The love that lasts is not
the earthly love.   It is a love of finer tissues
and stronger fibre, and it is eternal, being
hid with Christ in God.

Shall we not cling closer to that endless
love?   "O Love Divine, how sweet thou
art !"   Shall we not comfort ourselves with
the knowledge that we cannot be lost from
the clasping embrace of the everlasting arm
that fainteth not, neither is weary?   Shall
we not, by prayer, by study of God's Word,
by meeting with God's children, by faithful
service day by day, by use of the appointed
means of grace, and by frequent comtempla-
tion, dwell more than ever in the blessed-
ness of a life of entire trust, in the confidence of the Father's enduring love?

And now let me give you a bit of a song,
to sweeten the day, when you are tired.
The song is one with a history, for we are
told that it was sung in the rocks and caves
of France, three hundred years ago, during
the fierce persecutions of the Huguenots,
those persecutions which inspired Milton's
fine sonnet.

"Avenge, O Lord, thy slaughtered saints"
This is the hymn.   I love it, and so will you.

> I have a friend so precious,
>   So very dear to me,
> He loves me with such tender love,
>   He loves so faithfully,

I could not live apart from him,
  I love to feel him nigh,
And so we dwell together,
  My Lord and I.

Sometimes I'm faint and weary,
  He knows that I am weak,
And as he bids me lean on him,
  His help I gladly seek ;
He leads me in the paths of light
  Beneath a sunny sky,
And so we walk together,
  My Lord and I.

He knows how much I love him,
  He knows I love him well,
But with what love he loveth me
  My tongue can never tell ;
It is an everlasting love
  In ever rich supply,
And so we love each other,
  My Lord and I.

I tell him all my sorrows,
  I tell him all my joys,
I tell him all that pleases me,
  I tell him what annoys ;
He tells me what I ought to do,
  He tells me what to try,
And so we talk together,
  My Lord and I.

He knows how I am longing
  Some weary soul to win,
And so he bids me go and speak
  The loving word for him ;
He bids me tell his wondrous love,
  And why he came to die,
And so we work together,
  My Lord and I.

I have his yoke upon me,
   And easy 'tis to bear;
In the burden which he carries
   I gladly take a share;
For then it is my happiness
   To have him always nigh—
We bear and yoke together,
   My Lord and I.

A thoughtful woman has said a true word
for the old as follows :

"Those of us who have come near to the
western mountain, behind which the sun is
slowly but surely setting, know how natural
it is to sit down in the late afternoon and
take a backward turn of travel.   Miles have
been passed over since the fresh young
morning.   There were shadowy places and
dark vales of sorrow to pass through, chilly
winds to face, and storms that beat hard
enough to leave the weatherworn marks on
the heart and face.   But why travel over
the hard paths so often, instead of the pleasant ways through which we journeyed?
surely there were many sunshiny days,
flowers growing by the green wayside, and
beautiful calms after the terrible storms.
God's hospices of rest seemed to come just
at the very place where we thought we were
so weary that we could not take another
step.

Every day that we live we may make life
harder for others by telling over and over
our sorrows and disappointments, or we
may make life easier by entering into the

interest of those who are coming behind us, and giving cheery words instead of whiney, discouraging sounds whenever we come to a new turn in the road.

By living in a quiet, patient, cheerful way, we shall teach the sweet lesson of trust in the Lord and faith in Him, showing by our lives that we believe that the paths through which He has led us were the ones He, in His wisdom, chose for us. When we feel oppressed with the sorrows that have encompassed our way, and miss the dear ones who were our companions, but who have passed on beyond the gates, there is one person to whom we can go and talk it all over. Christ's humanity makes Him very dear to us. He knows our sorrows and He will help us bear them. When we come from those quiet talks alone with Him, we have brighter faces and sweeter words for the dear ones with whom we live.

Equally sensible and very suggestive is the little incident which is next related.

A bright woman, when applauded recently for her goodness, begged her friend to let the matter drop. "For," she said, whimsically, "though I do try to be good from some really high motives, yet I have one reason for trying which I am afraid is a low one." "What do you mean?" inquired her laughing friend. "I mean that I once heard, many years ago, that beauty after fifty depended not on features, but on char-

acter. Like all women, I desired to be
beautiful, and as Providence has denied me
the 'features' necessary to secure that result in early life, I determined to make the
attempt to be beautiful at fifty.  1 am
eighty-five now," she concluded, merrily,
"and I must confess that I see no signs of
this Indian-summer loveliness, but I still
try to be good."

These friends treated the matter as a jest,
but there is really sense and truth in the
saying that beauty in later life, in either
man or woman, is dependent upon character far more than upon form and color.
It is a common experience for a young
woman to say : "How fine looking Mrs.
—— is.  She must have been a beautiful
girl!"  And to hear the reply : "No, she
was not nearly as good-looking in her youth
as she is now.  Her beauty has developed
with her years."  And it may have been
observed that this is the oftenest true of
women of high character.  Nobility will
tell upon the outward aspect.  The carriage
of the figure, the pose of the head, the expression of the face—these come to reveal
more and more, with the lapse of time, the
inner life.  There is something more than a
mere pretty sentiment intended in that part
of "The Little Minister," where we read of
the beautiful face that God gives to all who
love Him and follow His commandments.
Unselfishness,   sincerity,   thoughtfulness,

refinement—all of these graces of character which are worth so much more than mere outward shape and color—lend their charm to those who have consistently cherished them, until at fifty they may really become beautiful.

Scant beauty nature gave her ; in disguise,
  Rugged and harsh she bade her go about
With face unlovely, save the dark, sad eyes,
  From which her fearless soul looked bravely out.

But Life took up the chisel, used her face
  Roughly, with many blows, as sculptors use a block ;
It wrought a little while, and, lo, a grace
  Fell, as a sunbeam falls upon a rock.

Across her soul a heavy sorrow swept,
  As tidal waves sweep sometimes o'er the land,
Leaving her face, when back it ebbed and crept,
  Tranquil and purified, like tide-washed sand.

And of her face her gentleness grew part,
  And all her holy thoughts left there their trace,
A great love found its way within her heart,
  Its root was there, its blossom in her face.

So when death came to set the sweet soul free
  From the poor body that was never fair,
We watched her face and marvelled much to see
  How Life had carved for Death, an angel there.

Not a bad idea is this one, of keeping what we may call a "pleasure book," and setting down in it daily all the interesting happenings, the unexpected bits of sunshine, and the little breaks which make up the delight of living. I heard not long ago of a woman, who said, "I have a book for every year since I left school, and a place for every day. It is but a little thing—the new gown, the chat with a friend, the thoughtfulness of the husband, a flower, a book, a walk in the field, a letter, a concert or a drive ; but it all goes into my Pleasure Book ; and when I am inclined to fret I have only to read a few pages to see what a happy, blessed woman I am. You may see my treasures if you will."

Slowly the fretful acquaintance turned over the pages of the book her friend brought her, reading a little here and there. One day's entries ran thus : "Had a pleasant letter from Mother. Saw a beautiful lily in a window. Found a pin I thought I had lost. Saw such a bright, happy girl on the street. Husband brought some roses in the evening."

Bits of verse and lines from her daily reading have gone into the Pleasure Book of this world-wise woman, until its pages are a storehouse of truth and beauty.

"Have you found a pleasure for every day ?"

"For every day," the low voice answered ; "I had to make my theory come true, you know."

## THE MONEY BAG.

If home life is to be perfectly smooth and free from friction, the management of the joint income must be put upon a basis of entire confidence and perfect justice. The honored wife, "who has free access to the money, will not be half so likely to lavish it as the woman who is put off with scanty and infrequent sums. She who knows how much there is to spend will almost invariably keep within the limits. If she does not know, her imagination will be very likely to magnify the fountain, and if but meagre supplies are forthcoming, she will attribute it to niggardliness, and will consider everything that can be got from her husband as legal plunder ; and with underground pipes and above-ground trenches it shall go hard but she will drain him tolerably dry. Then he will inveigh against her extravagance, and so not only lose his money, but his temper, his calmness, and his complacency, all the while blaming her when the fault is chiefly his own. If he had but frankly acquainted her with the main facts ; if he had but permitted her to look in and see what was the capacity of the reservoir, instead of leaving her to sit under the walls, knowing nothing of its resources but what she could learn from the occasional spouting of a single small pipe, he would have avoided all the trouble.   It is so rarely that a wife will recklessly transcend her reasonable income, that I do not think it worth while to suggest any provision against the evil.   It is an abnormal and sporadic case, to be treated physiologically rather than philosophically.   The man has unfortunately allied himself to a mad woman, or he has found to his regret that there is nothing more fulsome than a she-fool."

Many husbands, otherwise admirable men and excellent citizens, have an erroneous impression that the money they bestow upon their wives is a gratuity on their part. They earn ; their wives spend in their view, and they altogether fail to see that the wife's part in the administration is as important as their own in the production.

In point of fact, the wife is just as much a producer as the husband.   Her part in the concern is just as important as his.   She earns it as truly, and has just as strong a claim and just as much a right to it as he ; if possible she has more, for she ought to receive some compensation for the gap that yawns between work and wages.   It is much more satisfactory to receive the latter as a direct result of the former, than as a kind of alms.   Many a woman does as much to build up her husband's prosperity as he does himself. Many a woman saves him from failure and disgrace. And, as a general rule, the fate and fortunes of the family lie in her hands as much as in his. What absurdity to *pay* him his *wages* and to *give* her money to go shopping with!

A woman who went around to make a collection for a small local charity, told me that she could not help noticing the difference between the married and the unmarried women. The latter took out their purses on the spot and gave their mite or mint without hesitation. The former parleyed and would see about it, gave rather uncertainly, and must speak to Edward before they could decide. Now it may well be that a woman who has only her own self to provide for can give more liberally than one upon whose purse come the innumerable requisitions of a family. The mother may be forced to make many sacrifices, and yet be so blessed in the making that there shall be no sacrifice.

A married woman should know with accuracy the extent and resources of the family exchequer. If the money is a salary, regularly paid on an appointed day, there will be little difficulty in its appropriate division and apportionment. If, on the contrary, it is a fluctuating income, still let the wife and the daughters know what they may properly spend, and do away with heart-burnings,

18

discord, and painful scenes, which have their origin in fusses and quarrels over domestic finance. There is really no reason "why a married woman should hesitate, or be embarrassed, or consult Edward as to the expenditure of a dime or a dollar, any more than an unmarried one. There may be more calls on the purse, but she ought to be mistress of it. She ought to know her husband's circumstances well enough to know what she can afford to give away, and she ought to be as free to use her judgment as he is to use his. In any unusual emergency, each will wish to consult the other; but he does not think of asking her as to the disposal of every chance quarter of a dollar, neither should she think of asking him. If circumstances make it necessary to sail close to the wind, sail close to the wind; but let both be in the same boat.

If one might judge from the newspapers, extravagance is a peculiarity of women. So far as my observation goes, the extravagance of women is not for a moment to be compared with the extravagance of men. A man is perversely, persistently, and with malice aforethought, extravagant. He is extravagant in spite of admonition and remonstrance. Where his personal comfort or interest is concerned, he scorns a sacrifice. He laughs at the suggestion that such a little thing makes any difference one way or another. He has not even the idea of economy. He does not know what the word means. He does not know the thing when he sees it. Women take to it naturally. A certain innate sense of harmony keeps them from being wasteful. Their extravagance is the exception, not the rule. They are willing to incur self-denial. They do not scorn to take thought and trouble, and be put to inconvenience, for the sake of saving money. The greater animalism of man also comes out here in full force. If sacrifice must be, a woman will sacrifice her comforts before her taste. The man will let his tastes go, and keep his comforts, and call it good sense. A woman's extravagance is to some purpose. A man's to none. She buys many dresses, but she gives her old ones away, or cuts them over for the children, and works dextrously."

The very fact that a woman's whole life obliges her to concern herself with small and often very trifling matters of detail, assists her to be economical, frugal, to watch narrowly for ways and means of saving. Trust her with the money-bag and she will not shame your foresight.

A certain amount of training in business methods, and a systematic keeping of accounts would go far to making home life pleasant. We cannot be happy where we are always on the rack. If we have been spending more than we ought, let us cut

down our expenses, but let husband and
wife come to a mutual understanding on the
subject and arrange matters according to
their united discretion.

## CORRESPONDENCE.

Everybody writes letters in these days, not such long, leisurely letters as our forefathers did, when postage was a matter of moment, but letters off-hand, to friends, to relatives, to strangers, to people on business, letters of ceremony, letters of invitation, letters of condolence, in short, letters on every occasion and touching every matter under the sun. We would hardly know how to carry on our modern life without correspondence.

Regarding the externals of this everyday function, the mere dress and machinery of letters, you need if you would be conformable to good rules, a supply of white smooth note paper, with envelopes to match it, a trustworthy pen, and black ink. The ink must not be pallid and diffident, as if afraid to show its face, and the pen must be a straightforward implement, warranted neither to blot nor to spatter at the foot of a page, thus injuring both the letter and the writer's temper. It is an easy matter to provide one's self and the house with the right sort of stationery, yet we have all been in homes where there was only one pen, and that kept on a shelf behind the sitting-room clock, and where a sheet of paper was a luxury very hard to obtain at short notice.

Each person old enough to read and write ought to have an individual supply of note paper and individual pens and ink. For the little children, fanciful papers with designs of brownies and kelpies, or rosebuds and ferns, may do very nicely, but let all grown-up people eschew every style except that which is severery plain.

An engraved heading is permitted or a monogram, for, when a lady or a gentleman has a very large correspondence, time is saved by having the town, or the street and number all plainly stated at the top of one's sheet, but beyond this, have no decoration, and avoid rough edges, tinted papers, and everything in the least savoring of eccentricity.

In letters of business, be brief, pointed and explicit. Let the date be clearly written at the top of the page under the address, which should always be given in full. In letters of friendship which are informal, it is now customary to write the date at the end instead of the beginning of the letter.

Sign your name in full, and very legibly. It is very vexatious to read a letter through and then find the writer's signature vague and indistinct.

Some years ago, a lady of New York,

spending sometime abroad, chanced upon a work written in German, by a member of the nobility. She was so pleased with this volume that she translated it for her own satisfaction and that of a few friends, and I quote from it some eminently suggestive observations about the style of women's letters. The high-born German lady thinks that the interval between the receipt of a letter and its reply should, at its longest, be never more than four weeks. I myself think that two weeks is a better interval in a regular and friendly correspondence, though members of a household temporarily separated may prefer to write to one another every day. Friends residing at a distance, and meeting only semi-occasionally, may avoid the danger of drifting apart by a periodical exchange of letters which may keep each in touch and in intimate knowledge of the other and her affairs.

If one receives regularly every month news from a friend—I mean, of course, such news as I have in mind—then no alienation can arise between friends who are separated ; they can meet after ten years of separation and be bound together in the same way as when they parted. They can in truth go on together in spirit, and their exchange of letters may prove the greatest blessing to them.

Naturally, the blessing will be increased if circumstances allow the space of time to be reduced. More frequent or even daily writing has the same disadvantage as unfrequent writing. Namely, at a great distance we cannot wait for the answer to our last letter. This constant crossing of letters makes the correspondence very unpleasant. One asks questions which have been accidentally answered by the other before receiving our letter. One explains something with great trouble and expense of time without knowing that the receiver has already heard it all from another source. One is grieved, angry and anxious about a thing which has already been arranged and settled. In a word, misunderstandings of all kinds arise, and much time for writing is unnecessarily lost, if we do not await the answer to our last letter before writing another. Such hasty exchange of letters can be compared to the struggle between two angry adversaries, who both speak at the same time without listening to hear what the other is saying.

Let every one have his say out in writing as well as in speaking, and afterward you may answer them.

We will set aside the daily letters of a tenderly attached couple who are engaged, or the case of the family of a sick person whose loved ones at a distance cannot rest without receiving daily news.

Bnt we, who live in the ordinary manner, can wait until the time comes which we have set aside for correspondence with our distant loved ones. We take their last letter out of the portfolio, read it through once, and then we begin our letter by comprehensively answering every question; we take especial pains to do this in cases where inquiries have been made about the health of our dear ones, about events in the family or village life, and we tell in our own turn, what items of interest we may, taking care to think of those particulars which our friends will most enjoy.

How shall one tell these things?

"Just as one would speak." That is the only good, authentic rule for familiar letters.

Discard everything as nonsense which you have learned and read about the arrangement and division of sentences, about style, etc., banish all printed letters of celebrated persons from your memory, do not attempt anything, do not strive after any model, be yourself in your letters, and you will succeed well; they will not be compositions, they will not be models of style, but they will be veritable letters.

Think of the persons to whom you write and imagine they are beside you, and tell them simply with your pen what you would tell them with your lips.

The habit of constantly placing before us the person to whom we write, is one of the principal requisites of pleasing, interesting, and speaking letters. After the first few

lines we must forget entirely that we are
writing, and we must only be occupied in
mute speech and visible thought. While
the words are flying over the paper, we must
see a joyful smile beam on the face of the
dear one far away, we must see them start
with incredulous astonishment or listen with
increasing interest. We must see the tears
come into their faithful eyes, and hasten to
breathe a word of comfort before the pain
which we have occasioned reaches a crisis.
During the hours which we devote to such
a letter, we must detach ourselves from other
thoughts, and give ourselves wholly and
singly to the matter in hand. Some very
simple-hearted and imperfectly educated
people are models of good letter-writing,
because they do let themselves out thoroughly and completely in the correspondence they carry on with those they love.
One may describe anything in a letter, according to the person to whom it is sent.

To one you would describe a pretty *fête
champêtre*, to another a grand entertainment; to this one I would comment on my
children, while to another I would speak of
what I had been reading, or of some kind
of woman's or household work, or touch
hastily upon whatever subject I would speak
of if I were talking with my absent friend.

Those who go through the world with
their eyes open may be sure that their life
will not flow on in such an uniform, un-

eventful way that they will have no material
for writing, or even lack of time, and these
two things should never be offered as excuses
for long silence.

Who is not familiar with the following
form : " I would willingly write more, but
I cannot think of anything interesting to
tell you ; " " What can I tell you, for nothing
has happened of the least importance ; "
" My letter is very short to-day, but I have
searched in vain for a subject to lengthen it.
I find in reading it over that it is very
stupid," etc.

I would urge every one who uses such
phrases in writing to abandon them instantly, for it would be so much better to leave
the last page of the letter empty.

When one has nothing to say it were better to remain silent ; this is a golden rule
which applies as well to the pen as to the
lips.

If one does not wish to let the regular
post-day pass without sending some news,
we have now the excellent introduction of
postal cards. Since the invention of postal
cards it is quite unnecessary to send letters
which contain absolutely nothing.

One can write, " All are well with us.
There is nothing new. Heartfelt greetings."
In this way friends receive expected news
and are much more gratified than by a couple
of pages of empty words.

The much-loved " no subject to write

about" or "no time," are, without doubt, in ninety-nine cases, only empty excuses. I assert that in order to write good letters only one thing is necessary, the will to do it.

As regards a familiar correspondence, the so-called journal letters are an excellent arrangement. It is a very good plan and much to be recommended to write a little every day, and at the end of the week or month to send the letter. Sometimes it is hard to find time to write a long, continuous letter at once, or one cannot give one's self up to writing on the post-day, but by writing a little each day the letter is ready before the time. When one writes something each day it is not so easy to forget an event or a remark which, perhaps, would be overlooked later by the pressure of more important events.

Alas! it must be owned that in too many instances persons who write letters have not studied in them the art of being agreeable. Have you never seen anything like this?

First page, Excuses for the long silence; second page, Thanks for the last letter, without any remarks on its contents; third page, Excuse that one is obliged to close one's letter, although there is so much to relate; fourth page, Compliments and greetings, wishes for one's health, hopes for an immediate answer; postscript, Remarks about the bad writing, which are excused on account of the haste of the writer.

Such is the stereotyped style of thousands and more than thousands of women's letters, which are daily flying around the world. One regrets that so much paper, so much time, and so much postage should be wasted.

Speaking of postage, never forget to enclose return stamps if you are writing on your own business to some one who must answer your letter, at the cost of his own time, thought and pains. One or two stamps cost very little, but when one has a large correspondence, the tax of postage is great, and courtesy absolutely requires this precaution at your hands.

Whatever else we do, let us not send hurt or grieved or angry letters, out of an impulse of wounded feeling, to any correspondent. For a written word is in a sense imperishable, and long after our first emotion of resentment has passed, our inscribed and perpetuated wrath may survive, to sting and burn and blight a sorrowing and penitent heart.

Letters of condolence should be sent very soon after hearing of a bereavement and should be tender and full, but not necessarily diffuse. The house of mourning is not a place for much speech. We may just say that we are sorry, that we commend our afflicted friend to the only Comforter, and that will be sufficient.

Letters of acknowledgment of favors received, of gifts and tokens of love, should be very spontaneous. Never be frugal of thanks. Above everything never procrastinate your thanks. Write at once and assure the giver that the gift was what you wanted, that it has brought you a joy, that you treasure it as an expression of esteem.

The bride answers with a note of thanks the wedding gifts which come to her; if possible doing this before the wedding and while she still bears her maiden name.

The child, in a home of courtesy and sweet graces, early learns to say, "I thank you," and we should keep the beautiful habit up all through our lives to the end. Thanks oil the rusty locks and keep them from grating. Thanks distinguish the bountiful man from the churl.

It is a sign of a meagre and half-developed nature to be too economical and sparing of thanks.

To say of a man or woman, "He or she writes a charming letter," is to describe one who may safely be trusted to adorn any society, however exalted.

## SOME CHARMING EXAMPLES.

Scattered through the pages of biography the diligent reader finds many bright examples of men and women who have illustrated in their careers the fine art of living agreeably. Of the idolized wife of the Rev. Charles Kingsley we are told that through her pure convincing faith she helped to mould the destiny of a great man. This is a life-work of which any woman may well be proud ; it is a married career of this unselfish kind which brings out those brilliant characteristics of a woman which otherwise might never be developed. As we think of Kingsley as a young man, unsettled by the difficulties attending religious belief, and then compare the winding up of his work on earth, as he preached in Westminster Abbey, on November 29th, 1874, we see the grand and complete consummation of those desires which his wife had cherished from the hour when she was thrown in contact with him.

Frederick Denison Maurice, a man whose influence was potential with epoch-making men, and whose name is yet held in great reverence in England was, before his marriage, given to isolation, self-restraint, reserve and a very marked silence.

It was indeed an important change which his marriage with Anna Barton produced, for she, it would seem, yearned for some loving sympathetic spirit upon which to lean—not having been content or happy in her life at home. Happily they met— exactly suited as they were for each other ; and in her society Denison found a wife who was good and true ; her intense openness and veracity being a marked feature of her character.

"She was the most transparently truthful person I ever knew," was commonly said of her ; "the most fresh and informal." She was possessed, too, "of a particular kind of humor, of which she was full, and it not unfrequently expressed itself somewhat epigrammatically, but the humor was almost always the serving up of facts, so to say, in their own broth."

Sir Samuel Romilly, writing of Lady Romilly, his beloved wife, thus describes her, and incidentally throws a side-light on himself as a most agreeable husband. Alluding to his first meeting with her, as a bright young girl, he says :

"I saw in her the most beautiful and accomplished creature that ever blessed the sight and understanding of man. A most intelligent mind, an uncommonly correct judgment, a lively imagination, a cheerful disposition, a noble and generous way of thinking, an elevation and heroism of character, and a warmth and tenderness of affection such as is rarely found even in her sex, were among her extraordinary endowments. I was captivated alike by the beauties of her person and the charms of her mind. A mutual attachment was formed between us, which at the end of little more than a year was consecrated by marriage.

"All the happiness I have known in her loved society, all the many and exquisite enjoyments which my dear children have afforded me, even my extraordinary success in my profession, the labors of which, if my life had not been so cheered and exhilarated I never could have undergone—all are to be traced to this unexpected and seemingly accidental meeting."

When this admirable woman and adored wife died, her husband could not live without her and survived her only three days.

The wife of Sir William Hamilton, who was a famous scholar and writer, helped her husband by acting as his amanuensis, and for some years wrote at his dictation whenever he needed her assistance. Cheerful and buoyant, she rallied him when he was gloomy, and depression fled before her loving ministrations. More and more as years went on and his strength declined, and illness attacked him, did he lean upon her and seek to have her constantly beside him, and with

ever-increasing care and assiduity did she to
the last moment fulfil her life's labor of love
—to smooth and cheer and remove all outward hindrances from the path of her husband ; feeling when she could no longer do
this that her occupation was gone. She had
the only reward for which she cared in the
one life which she and her husband in their
several spheres lived, in the perfect confidence which he reposed in her, in the
depths of his affection and appreciation.

Naturally, too, of an indolent disposition,
much of Sir William Hamilton's work would
have been left undone had it not been for
the influence of his wife. She had the
happy power of keeping him up to what he
had to do, sustaining and helping him forward by her cheerful, energetic force of character.   It was by her power of guidance
and counsel, and by that "womanly tact
which can thread its way through difficulties
where mere intelligence is baffled," that he
was enabled to accomplish what he actually
did in literature and philosophy.

Thomas Hood, writing to his wife, exclaimed, "I never was anything, dearest,
till I knew you, and I have been a better,
happier, and more prosperous man ever
since. Lay by that truth in lavender, dearest, and remind me of it when I fail."

Quite recently J. M. Barrie, in his sur-
passingly tender and beautiful tribute to his
mother, "Margaret Ogilvy," draws a por-

trait of a woman who, her life long, from youth to old age, was winningly agreeable. A similar picture is sketched by a firm hand in Ian Maclaren's "Beside the Bonny Brier-bush," in his character of Marget Howe.

Our own dear Mrs. Prentiss whose "Stepping Heavenward" is a Christian classic, has left us abundant evidence that she knew how to sweeten life, and make its flavor agreeable. To a young friend, this busy woman, and pastor's wife and help-meet said one day : "I was right sorry to lose your Saturday's call. It was a happy day to me, but I can conceive of no enjoyment of any sort that would put me out of sympathy with the trials of friends :

> " 'Old and young are bringing troubles,
>   Great and small, for me to hear;
> *I have often blessed my sorrows
>   That drew others' grief so near.'*

"I thought I was saying a very ordinary thing when I spoke of thanking God for His long years of discipline, but very likely life did not look to me at your age as it does now. I was rather startled the other day, to find it written in German, in my own hand, 'I cannot say the will is there,' referring to a hymn which says, 'Der Will ist da, die Kraft ist klein, Doch wird dir nicht zuwider seyn.' I suppose there was some great struggle going on when this foolish heart said that, just as if God did not *invariably* do for us the very best that can be done. You speak of having your love to Jesus intensified by interviews with me. It can hardly be otherwise, when those meet together who love Him, and it is a rule that works both ways; acts and reacts. I should be thankful if no human being could ever meet me, even in a chance way, and not go away clasping Him the closer, and if I could meet no one who did not so stir and move me. It is my constant prayer. I have such insatiable longings to know and love Him better that I go about hungering and thirsting for the fellowship of those who feel so too; when I meet them I call them my 'benedictions.' Next best to being with Christ Himself, I love to be with those who have His spirit and are yearning for more of His likeness. You speak of putting 'deep and dark chasms between' yourself and Christ. He lets us do this that we may learn our nothingness, our weakness, and turn, disgusted, from ourselves to Him. May I venture to assure you that the 'chasms' occur less and less frequently as one presses on, till finally they turn into 'mountains of light.' Get and keep a will for God, and everything that will is ready for will come. This is about a tenth part of what I might say."

This strikes the note of a high and hallowed Christian courage; one who dwells near the Master in hallowed fellowship and communion may write thus. The finest and loveliest lessons for life are taught in Christ's school. Only those who sit at His feet may learn how to live divinely in a storm-tossed world.

Dr. Prentiss spoke of the weeks just preceding her death, when neither of them had a thought that it was near, as indescribably lovely and beautiful. They had gone to their summer home at Dorset, Vermont.

"For four or five weeks after coming here she was very much occupied about the house, and seemed rather weary and careworn. But the pressure was then over and she had leisure for her flowers and her painting, for going to the woods with the girls, and for taking her favorite drives with me. She spoke repeatedly of you and other friends. On the 23d of July I started for Monmouth Beach. The week preceding this little journey was one of the happiest of our married life. No words can tell how sweet and loving and bright—in a word, how just like herself—she was. The impression of that week accompanied me to the sea-side and continued with me during my whole stay there. As day after day I sat looking out upon the ocean, or walked alone up and down the shore, she was still in all my thoughts. The noise of the breakers, the boundless expanse of waters, the passing ships, going out and coming in, recalled similar scenes long ago on the coast of Maine, before and after our marriage—scenes with which her image was indissolubly blended. Then I met old friends and found new ones, who talked to me with grateful enthusiasm of 'Stepping Heavenward,' 'More Love to Thee, O Christ,' and other of her writings. In truth, my feelings about her, while I was at Monmouth Beach, were quite peculiar and excite my wonder still. I scarcely know how to describe them. They were at times very intense, and, I had almost said, awe-struck, seemed bathed in a sweet Sabbath stillness, and to belong rather to the other world than to this of time and sense. How do you explain this? Was my spirit, perhaps, touched in some mysterious way by the coming event? Certainly, had I been warned that she was so soon to leave me, I could hardly have passed those days of absence in a mood better attuned to that in which I now think of her as forever at home with the Lord."

The indispensable requisites to being a charming and agreeable person are tact, unselfishness and sympathy. One must have these. He who possesses the capacity of expressing active sympathy walks like an angel among his grateful fellowmen and scatters the roses of happiness along the sorrowful way of life from which none are exempt, while thousands of men

do not understand how to pluck them from
the thorn-hedges which infest their way. If
anywhere sympathy is related to love to
such a degree that they may be confounded
with each other, it is in the form of soft,
gentle sympathy which never becomes
weary, and never spares itself in searching
out opportunities, and only works the more
diligently and bestows the greater blessings,
when the means with which it works are
small and its circle is a narrow one. Its
efforts are only increased when convinced
that nothing it can do can lessen the danger
which threatens a beloved human life, and
that its efforts and strength are not adequate
really to help them.

There are such angels in the form of men,
whose only occupation in life is to shed
happiness about them unceasingly, by
simple means which attract no notice, and
when I have met such heavenly messengers,
they have almost always been—old women,
with the rare above-mentioned exceptions.
Let me tell you of one.

Near to the seventies and with a weak,
delicate body, this lady has known how to
retain a freshness and clearness of spirit and
heart, and though by the world she was
regarded as an old woman thirty years ago,
she still remains young. She has brought
up a numerous family in the most faithful and
self-denying manner, and now not only her
own grown-up children, but even her grand

children and great-grand children seek her help and counsel in all difficult circumstances. And she is also for a larger circle of beloved friends of every age and sex, the mild, friendly angel of comfort, the thoughtful counsellor, and the ready helper. She is the counsellor of each one, and all great and small troubles are confidently brought to her, for relief and consolation. For years this dear old matron was the trusted counsellor and adviser of young men at college, her own sons and grandsons and their comrades, and in her old age she yet retains their affectionate regard.

Most of them have become happy fathers of families, and even now nothing more beautiful can be seen than the touching devotion and gratitude which they all retain for their former adopted mother. If any one of these professors or doctors who are scattered through the whole world, comes near to her place of residence, he willingly travels a whole night that he may spend a couple of hours with her. He enters with the old greeting, "Good-day, mamma;" he takes her in his arms, and the beloved old eyes overflow with joy and pride that "Adolphus," "Francis," or "Henry," are so well, for these stately bearded gentlemen have always remained such to her. Without ceremony he sits down to the table, and while eating relates what has happened in his official life, as well as in his family circle.

But at last he draws his chair nearer to her and begins : "Do you know, mamma, I come with a request." And when the request has been discussed to the satisfaction of both parties, they recall again the pleasant old days. And as this "mamma," the old name being still given, is in correspondence with all her adopted children, she can give information on every subject ; and more than once she hears them say, "Of course, I owe all that to you," or, "What would have become of me if you had not been there, mamma!" The conversation becomes more interesting, until at last the adopted son jumps up, exclaiming in dismay: "Dear me, I shall lose my train." They all still remain in such relations as these to the old "mamma." Perhaps some one of them may smile when he reads these words, but they will admit it all, and will never forget what they owe to the quiet, simple old lady, or for how much they have to thank her.

I can only remark, as often as I hear complaints in regard to the unrestrained behavior of the youth of our day, that the fault in great measure lies in this : There are no longer any old ladies.

When we fail to find charming and interesting old women in our social assemblies, society is in a state of decadence indeed. But young women are now busy in making the old women of the future, and they have

it in their power to mould them as they
choose.

In the " Life of the Rev. John McElhenny,"
an aged Presbyterian minister, long settled
in West Virginia, we find a graceful picture
of such a gentlewoman as presiding over a
household, makes it a type of heaven.

A grandchild tells of the manse with its
ample living-room, wainscoted in cherry,
and lighted by four large windows, answering to parlor, bedchamber and modern
dining-room.   Here the pastor and his wife
had raised a family of five children, and
there they now sat in the evening of a long
and well-spent life, over which a lengthened
twilight was yet to shed its glow.

" Heart to heart they had passed through
mingled scenes of joy and sorrow, and hand
to hand they were to glide down the evening
of life together !

" Children's children made their hearts
young again, and before the old minister
was called hence his hand had been laid
in benediction upon a child of the fourth
generation.   And who can doubt that the
blessing was fulfilled, when the lad's brief
span was run, and the boy of promise went
to meet him before God's throne ?

" My grandmother was a notable housekeeper, and her hands bore the traces of a
busy and energetic life.   She was a small,
brisk old woman, who looked well to the
ways of her household, never eating the

bread of idleness, although she had several handmaids at her service. Her loaves of salt-risen bread, and horehound syrup were famous in the community, and she never failed to provide the one or the other for a sick neighbor, as the occasion might call for. She was a lavish provider and generous to excess, much to the detriment of the minister's slender purse, and there are many entries against his "lady" in those early accounts which have fallen into my hands !

"Well do I remember the evening meal, the well-filled board, the early prayers which followed, the setting away of the tea things, and the general righting up of the living-room ! The housemaids were called in, the candles lighted in the tall brass candlesticks, the chairs drawn up, the well-worn Bible placed on a small stand, and the venerable dame seated opposite to her husband, ready to correct him if he faltered in a word.

"She knew the Bible by heart, and if, owing to insufficient light or failing eyesight, he stumbled over a word, the good lady would correct him in an audible whisper, to the suppressed mirth of two small grand-daughters present. It was her custom to read the Bible through once a year, following the old-fashioned method of five chapters daily, and seven on Sundays.

"Other than biblical lore she had at her tongue's end. She could recite "Cowper's Task," from beginning to end, the ballad of

John Gilpin, and various Revolutionary
ballads and patriotic odes."

From our own circles of kindred, from
our own friends and neighbors, we may cull
beautiful examples, specimens worth preserv-
ing in memory of the art of being agreeable
to those whom we meet on the journey of
life.

## THE VERY BEST.

Assuredly there is a time when it is right not to be agreeable, even though there is never a time to be disagreeable. But, friends, we may well remember that there arise crises when the brave word must be spoken at any cost. Truth must not be sacrificed on the altar of a compromising insincerity. To the Christian heart, there must always stand foremost the desire to serve the Master, and when His Name is assailed, when the Lord's Day is assaulted, whenever and wherever profanity or wickedness stalks before us, then must we gird on our armor, and be true to our colors, let the event be what it will.

It may sometimes be cowardly to smile and be silent, when bold standing for the right is imperatively demanded. Every one's conscience must decide in matters of this sort. Few men, in our day, have said more forceful words for the daily life than the Rev. J. R. Miller, and he pithily tells us that :

"There are degrees in virtue. All graces are not of equal value. Without the observance of the place and proportion of each, a distorted and ill-formed character must result. That man would be esteemed a foolish farmer who would put as much time and care upon the cultivation of his family flower-garden as upon his wheat-field. Similarly, it is a grievous error for any young person to consider all virtues alike. Symmetry of character is not to be developed in this way. We are bidden to covet earnestly the best gifts ; and, naturally, a merely good gift is not to be given equal rank with the best gifts.

"Patience, for instance, is a good virtue, an indispensable virtue ; but it is not supreme. Its nature is chiefly negative. To devote all one's attention to growing the grace of patience would in all likelihood insure a pleasant, but weak and unresisting character, submissive to wrongs that should not be borne, and inefficient in aggressive service.

"Courage excels patience. Strong, fearless hearts, that will dare and do anything for righteousness' sake, are more lacking in the world than patient hearts. Christ was patient, but he was also brave. His matchless courage stands out strong and luminous in his life. Down the ages his example sends the mighty message, "Be strong in the Lord." Without this spirit of unflinching and duty-doing courage, patience is ineffective. Eli was patient to the degree of over-indulgence ; therefore the brave son of Hannah was called to fill his place."

The desire to be popular may prove very misleading. It is well to be genial, fine of manner, lovable and beloved. It is well also to be honest, candid, responsible and noble. If possible combine these last qualities with a perfectly engaging and never-failing courtesy, and you come near arriving at the highest ideal type of manhood and of womanhood.

Says Bishop Brooks :

" In certain lands, for certain holy ceremonies, they prepare the candles with most anxious care. The very bees which distil the wax are sacred. They range in gardens planted with sweet flowers for their use alone. The wax is gathered by consecrated hands ; and then the shaping of the candles is a holy task, performed in holy places, to the sound of hymns, and in the atmosphere of prayers, All this is done because the candles are to burn in the most lofty ceremonies on most sacred days. With what care must the man be made whose spirit is to be the candle of the Lord ! It is his spirit which God is to kindle with Himself. Therefore the spirit must be the precious part of him. The body must be valued only for the protection and the education which the soul may gain by it. And the power by which his spirit shall become a candle is obedience. Therefore obedience must be the struggle and desire of his life ; obedience, not hard and forced, but ready,

loving, and spontaneous ; the obedience of
the child to the father, of the candle to the
flame ; the doing of duty not merely that
the duty may be done, but that the soul in
doing it may become capable of receiving
and uttering God ; the bearing of pain not
merely because the pain must be borne, but
that the bearing of it may make the soul able
to burn with the divine fire which found it
in the furnace ; the repentance of sin and
acceptance of forgiveness, not merely that
the soul may be saved from the fire of hell,
but that it may be touched with the fire of
heaven, and shine with the love of God, as
the stars, forever.

"Above all the pictures of life,—of what it
means, of what may be made out of it,—
there stands out this picture of a human
spirit burning with the light of the God whom
it obeys, and showing Him to other men.
O, my young friends, the old men will tell
you that the lower pictures of life and its
purposes turn out to be cheats and mistakes.
But this picture can never cheat the soul
that tries to realize it. The man whose life
is a struggle after such obedience, when at
last his earthly task is over, may look
forward from the borders of this life into the
other, and humbly say, as his history of the
life that is ended, and his prayer for the life
that is to come, The words that Jesus said—
'I have glorified Thee on the earth ; now,
O Father, glorify Me with Thyself forever.'"

The fine art of being agreeable shines out in our relations with organizations, with our church for example, and our benevolent society, and whenever we must act in concert with others. There is plenty of scope for the exercise of amicability, for yielding a little in non-essentials, for the piety which is sweet and Christ-like in these associations of men and women together.

Happy will it be for us, if our behavior is always consistent, if we never forget courtesy, if we are able to control our looks, our speech, and our actions, and ever have with us as a sweet aroma, the spirit of the highest charity.

'Twas in the night the manna fell
That fed the host of Israel.

Enough, for each day's fullest store
And largest need, enough, no more.

For wilful waste, for prideful show
God sent not angel's food below.

Still in our nights of deep distress
The manna falls our hearts to bless.

And, famished as we cry for bread,
With heavenly food our lives are fed.

And each day's need finds each day's store
Enough, dear Lord, what ask we more?

## FINE MANNERS.

I had occasion the other day to step into my kitchen to meet a man who had called to see whether I could engage him to attend to my furnace. I had no sooner stepped inside the door, than I recognized John as a man I had known some years ago ; an honest and hard-working mechanic who had married an excellent maid-of-all-work, who was also one of my humbler friends. As I went forward to meet John, he rose, advanced with his hand extended, and his homely countenance was lighted by a smile of genuine good feeling.

"It's yerself, mum," he said, "that's lookin' foine. Ye kapes your looks ! Foine and young ye do look ! "

Now, the art of conveying a compliment in a spontaneous and sincere way belongs to the very essence of good breeding. How much better I felt than I would have done had John shown by a surly indifference that I and my appearance were nothing to him. To so demean yourself that you make others pleased with you, and with themselves too, is to touch the summit of courtier-like gentleness of breeding.

Mrs. John Sherwood, an authority, in
" Manners and Social Usages" tells us that
" we do not want all the decent drapery of
life torn off ; we do not want to be told that
we are full of defects ; we do not wish
people to show us a latent antagonism ; and
if we have in ourselves the elements of
roughness, severity of judgment, a critical
eye which sees defects rather than virtues,
we are bound to study how to tone down
that native, disagreeable temper—just as we
are bound to try to break the icy formality
of a reserved manner, and to cultivate a
cordiality which we do not feel. Such a
command over the shortcomings of our own
natures is not insincerity, as we often find
that the effort to make ourselves agreeable
towards some one whom we dislike ends in
leading us to like the offending person. We
find that we have really been the offender,
going about with a moral tape-measure
graduated by ourselves, and measuring the
opposite party with a serene conceit which
has called itself principle or honor, or some
high-sounding name, while it was really
nothing but prejudice.

"We should try to carry entertainment
with us, and to seem entertained with our
company. A friendly behavior often con-
ciliates and pleases more than wit or bril-
liancy ; and here we come back to those
polished manners of the past, which were a
perfect drapery, and therefore should be

studied, and perhaps in a degree copied, by
the awkward and the shy, who cannot depend upon themselves for inspirations of
agreeability. Emerson says that "fashion
is good-sense entertaining company ; it
hates corners and sharp points of character ;
hates quarrelsome, egotistical, solitary, and
gloomy people ; hates whatever can interfere with total blending of parties, while it
values all particularities as in the highest
degree refreshing which can consist with
good-fellowship."

"It does the awkward and the shy good
to contemplate these words. It may not
immediately help them to become graceful
and self-possessed, but it will certainly have
a very good effect in inducing them to try.

"We find that the successful man of the
world has studied the temper of the finest
sword. He can bend easily, he is flexible,
he is pliant, and yet he has not lost the
bravery and power of his weapon. Men of
the bar, for instance, have been at the
trouble to construct a system of politeness,
in which even an offensive self-estimation
takes on the garb of humility. The harmony is preserved, a trial goes on with an
appearance of deference and respect, each
to the other, highly, most highly, commend-
able, and producing law and order where
otherwise we might find strife, hatred, and
warfare. Although this may be a mimic
humility, although the compliments may

be judged insincere, they are still the shadows of the very highest virtues. The man who is guarding his speech is ruling his spirit, is keeping his temper, that furnace of all afflictions, and the lofty chambers of his brain are cool and full of fresh air.

"A man who is by nature clownish, and who has what he calls, a "noble sincerity," is very apt to do injustice to the polished man ; he should, however, remember that the "manner of a vulgar man has freedom without ease, and that the manner of a gentleman has ease without freedom." A man with an obliging, agreeable address may be just as sincere as if he had the noble art of treading on everybody's toes. The "putter-down-upon-system" man is quite as often urged by love of display as by a love of truth; he is ungenerous, combative, and ungenial ; he is the "bravo of society."

"To some people a fine manner is the gift of nature. We see a young person enter a room, make himself charming, go through the transition period of boy to man, always graceful, and at man's estate aim to still possess that unconscious and flattering grace, that "most exquisite taste of politeness," which is a gift from the gods. He is exactly formed to please, this lucky creature, and all this is done for him by nature. We are disposed to abuse Mother Nature when we think of this boy's heritage of joy compared with her step-son, to whom she has given the burning blushes, the awkward step, the heavy self-consciousness, the uncourtly gait, the hesitating speech, and the bashful demeanor.

" But nothing would be omitted by either parent or child to cure the boy if he had a twisted ankle, so nothing should be omitted that can cure the twist of shyness, and therefore a shy young person should not be expected to confront such a trial.

"And to those who have the bringing up of shy young persons we commend these excellent words of Whately : 'There are many otherwise sensible people who seek to cure a young person of that very common complaint—shyness—by exhorting him not to be shy, telling him what an awkward appearance it has, and that it prevents his doing himself justice, but they do not always show him how he may improve himself.'"

To know what to do in a given situation adds very much to ease of deportment. Take the very familiar matter of introducing one friend to another. Everybody does not remember that you must present the younger to the older person, the gentleman to the lady, and speak the names of both with perfect distinctness. That is the whole secret of making a presentation, and it certainly is not difficult. In visiting one addresses one's hostess on arriving and bids her good-bye on leaving, and often at a

reception one can do little more. One is
not to be pardoned who is afraid to be
polite, or who fancies that boorish manners
are the symbol of sincerity and that polish
and refinement indicate affectation.

I have lately read again, and with a
pleasure so subtle and exquisite that I am
fain to share it with my friends and readers,
Tennyson's matchless Idyls of the King.
You recall King Arthur, the blameless king,
and his wonderful Round Table.

In that fair order of my Table Round,
A glorious company, the flower of men,
To serve as model for the mighty world,
And be the fair beginning of a time.
I made them lay their hands in mine and swear
To reverence the King, as if he were
Their conscience, and their conscience as their King,
To break the heathen and uphold the Christ,
To ride abroad redressing human wrongs,
To speak no slander, no, nor listen to it,
To lead sweet lives in purest chastity,
To love one maiden only, cleave to her,
And worship her by years of noble deeds,
Until they won her ; for indeed I knew
Of no more subtle master under heaven
Than is the maiden passion for a maid,
Not only to keep down the base in man,
But teach high thought, and amiable words
And courtliness, and the desire of fame,
And love of truth, and all that makes a man.

There are suggestions in that description for
you and for me.

In a family known to me the gentle older
sister sometimes reproves the boisterous

nursery troop by saying, "Hush-sh-sh, my children, your manners have not that repose which stamps the caste of Vere de Vere." The words are really a spell to conjure with, and straightway Mamie and Eddie try to be quieter and lovelier.

Said a lady not long since, "The true gentleman may wear broadcloth or fustian ; may carry a hod or a portfolio ; it matters not. Manners make the man." And the best of books gives us the golden rule to do as we would be done by, to love one another, the neighbor as one's self ; to emulate Christ, whose whole earthly career was one of service.

Purity of speech, the avoidance of silly and senseless slang, and of course the omission of everything which even trenches on the borders of profanity, will be regarded as imperative in those who would possess fine manners.

Nor must we force our views too strenuously on those who differ from us. The rule of moderation in our statements applies to our social converse. In matters of principle let us be firm without ostentation. In matters of transient importance, let us be forbearing and disposed to yield.

Politics are best left out of discussion at the dinner-table and the fireside unless people can fully control their tempers when engaged in a bout of argument with those on the opposite side.

Professor Ely in his treatise called "The Social Law of Service," tells us of two sisters whose manners were founded on a basis of Christian altruism. "These good women illustrated the motto on the title-page of the book in which is recorded the story of their lives : 'The glory of all glories is the glory of self-sacrifice.' At first sacrifice with them found a basis in asceticism. It was thought well-pleasing to God that they should deny themselves without any human motive or aim external to themselves. This early period of their history finds expression in many passages in the book. Sarah Grimké writes : 'I went to a meeting, and it being a rainy day I took a large, handsome umbrella which I had accepted from brother Henry, accepted doubtfully, therefore wrongfully, and have never felt quite easy to use it, which, however, I have done a few times. After I was in meeting I was much tried by a wandering mind, and every now and then the umbrella would come before me, so that I sat trying to wait on my God, and He showed me that I must not only give up this little thing, but return it to my brother.' After other reflections she adds, in a note : 'This little sacrifice was made. I sent the umbrella with an affectionate note to brother, and believe it gave him no offence to have it returned, and sweet has been the recompence, even peace.'

Even a very small bit of self-denial may

be glorified if done from a noble motive. Says the Rev. Frederick W. Robertson :

"Therefore come what may, hold fast to love. Though men should rend your heart, let them not embitter or harden it. We win by tenderness, we conquer by forgiveness. O ! strive to enter into something of that large celestial charity which is meek, enduring, unretaliating, and which even the overbearing world cannot withstand forever. Learn the new commandment of the Son of God. Not to love merely, but to love *as He loved.* Go forth in this spirit to your life duties ; go forth, children of the Cross, to carry everything before you, and win victories for God by the conquering power of a love like this."

To bring the heavenly down to the earthly, the ideal to the practical, don't let us have too much interference with our rights and privileges from acquaintances. Elderly people need to be cautioned as to their moods and manners in this particular. A suggestive article in a religious paper lately printed this moral :

"Edmund Burke when near the latter part of his life paid a tribute to the high and lovely character of his wife that is among the most beautiful and touching things in literature. In it he said, among other things, that her charm consisted not so much in the things she did as in the things she refrained from doing. The elderly person who

would be a welcome companion or guest in
the home, or with the young, must learn to
refrain from doing and saying many things.
The first great temptation to elderly people
is to want to direct in little, unimportant
things. No other characteristic—unless it
be fault-finding—will so quickly cause the
young to try to escape from the companionship of the old as this. Life with the young
is a series of experiments, and one of the
chief sources of enjoyment is the delightful
uncertainty that attends many of them. So,
unless young people are actually doing
wrong, it is a great deal better to let them
alone and let them find out things for themselves. The elderly person—grandfather,
grandmother, aunt or uncle, who proposes
to become a constant mentor to young people, will quickly find himself disliked. This
mentorship on the part of elderly people towards the young often takes the form of an
inquisitiveness that is peculiarly exasperating, especially when it is accompanied by a
running comment or criticism on the answers given. 'Children, where are you going?' just as they are starting off on some
expedition. 'To the woods! Well it looks
like rain and you would much better stay at
home in the yard ; it's foolish nonsense to
go and get your clothes wet and spoiled and,
take your deaths of cold.' 'Mary, why do
you wear that new dress every day ? If I
were your mother I would make you save

it for afternoons and church.' 'Willie, what are you whittling? A boat? It's all nonsense to make so many boats, and why don't you whittle in the barn and not on the porch?' The elderly person who indulges in such questioning and criticism will soon find that the children will instinctively 'edge off' when he comes around. No affection can blossom and unfold in the atmosphere of criticising inquisitiveness. The elderly person who can really play with children is possessed of a source of enjoyment second to none for the declining years of life. Its possession presupposes loving sympathy with children and consequently the power of making them happy, with its reflex influence of happiness conferred. With many elderly people this power of entering into the feelings of children—of being a child with them—is a natural gift. It has been a characteristic of some of the most eminent men and women. Lord Macaulay's favorite recreation, after a morning spent on his ponderous History, was to seek the house of his sister and play like a child with his little nephews and nieces. His entrance was a signal for uproarious joy and mirth. At once the sitting-room was the scene of all kinds of plays—the favorite one being 'Menagerie.' The sofa was pushed across the corner; Uncle Tom was lion or bear caged behind it and covered with newspapers. Or he was the wolf who talked to little Red Riding Hood; or the Mother Goose who made up rhymes for the little ones—rhymes that are positively unparalleled in merit by later rhymes for children. For the sake of these romps he declined many an invitation to stately dinner-parties, and he was rewarded with an affection on the part of his nephews and nieces such as few parents are blessed with. The elderly person who would bring this great blessing into his or her life may have to acquire the art of playing with children if it is not a natural gift. In order to do it he must become as a little child; must see things from a child's point of view. A well-known essayist is said to be preparing an essay on 'The Uses of Grandparents. Doubtless this will be one of them. Parents alas! too few have time to really play with the little ones; to dress dolls and then play with them; to make cats' cradles and whistles out of elderberry stalks in the spring—(what bought whistle could ever compare with the one that grandpa or uncle made?) to lead the gentle pony or kind old horse around the yard with all the little ones on his back; to make the 'teeter' board and then 'teeter' on it. These are the recreations practised with the little ones, that make the heart young and win for the old the tender and enduring affection of childhood and youth."

To all that has been said a word may be added about our voices too. We Americans are accused of having harsh nasal voices, of sacrificing sweetness and melody to a shrill tendency, to a scream or a shout. We need to cultivate full, round tones ; the sweet and silver voice is far more agreeable than the loud, harsh one. Temperament is revealed in the voice, sympathy vibrates in its chords. A brave woman bearing a great grief with outward calm may yet have "tears in her voice." Children, reproved in loud and un-modulated tones, themselves speak rudely. The voice indicates refinement or the reverse.

"'I dislike to have Wilthorpe come to see me,' said a very shy woman ; 'I know my voice will squeak so.' With her Wilthorpe, who for some reason drove her into an agony of shyness, had the effect of making her talk in a high, unnatural strain, excessively fatiguing.

"The presence of one's own family, who are naturally painfully sympathetic, has always had upon the bashful and the shy a most evil effect.

"'I can never plead a cause before my father.' 'Nor I before my son,' said two distinguished lawyers. 'If mamma is in the room, I shall never be able to get through my part,' said a young amateur musician."

Our manners are a part of our very natures. They cannot be put off and on like our clothes. They begin in our cradles and accompany us to our graves. We shall carry them with us to the next life, and wear them in the presence of the angels on high. So they are worth our constant thought and sedulous cultivation.

> " Who seeks the fadeless beauty
> Must seek for the use that seals
> To the grace of a constant blessing
> The beauty that use reveals.
> For into the folded robe alone
> The moth with its blighting steals."

Of a fascinating great lady of a former period we are told that beauty "constituted her smallest pretension to universal admiration; nor did it consist, like that of the Gunnings, in regularity of features and faultless formation of limbs and shape : it lay in the amenity and graces of her deportment, in her irresistible manners, and the seduction of her society. Her hair was not without a tinge of red ; and her face, though pleasing, yet, had it not been illuminated by her mind, might have been considered as an ordinary countenance. In addition to the external advantages which she had received from nature and fortune, she possessed an ardent temper, susceptible of deep as well as strong impressions ; a cultivated understanding, illuminated by a taste for poetry and the fine arts ; much sensibility, not exempt, perhaps, from vanity and coquetry." Wherever she went her influence was felt.

We shall not go far wrong if only we think it worth our while to be always agreeable.  I have seen colored people in the South, ignorant, poor, and lately freed from bondage, whose manners and tones and willingness to oblige made them models of behavior, and delightful personages.  I have met with rare courtesy from Irish peasants.  Politeness may belong to the most illiterate.  It is the fine embroidery in the robes of the most highly endowed. Without it no one will be a pleasant comrade on the road of life.   And

> "It isn't the thing you do, dear,
>   It's the thing you leave undone,
> That gives you a bit of a heartache
>   At the setting of the sun."

So, it is the part of wisdom to avoid sins of omission, as well as sins of commission, in this complex art of living harmoniously with our kith and kin, our neighbors and our friends.